For conference information
please write:
Evangelism Ministries
International Headquarters
6401 The Paseo
Kansas City, MO 64131

Today's Disciple

Discipleship Series

Fourth Edition

By W. Donald Wellman
Edited by David J. Felter

Beacon Hill Press of Kansas City
Kansas City, Missouri

Copyright 1996

Nazarene Publishing House

ISBN 083-411-6537
Printed in the
United States of America

10   9   8   7   6   5

DEDICATED
to the establishment and preservation of the belief
that the Spirit-filled life may be
UNDERSTOOD, EXPERIENCED, and SHARED
by the earnest believer in this present day.

We are deeply indebted to the following men
for their unselfish sharing and valued contribution
to the editing of this fourth edition:
Roger L. Clay
Ralph Earle
Harvey E. Finley
William Greathouse
Roger Hahn
Donald S. Metz
Jesse Middendorf
J. Fred Parker
W. T. Purkiser
Randall Smith
Robert Smith
Timothy L. Smith
W. Donald Wellman
Keith Wright

Contents

Preface

The discipling concept is not new. A disciple is a pupil, a follower, or an adherent of any teacher or school of religion, learning, or art (Webster). Great teachers have always had disciples. Great causes have always necessitated both disciples and disciplers.

Jesus Christ is the personification of the greatest cause ever revealed to humankind. He has had dedicated disciples in the past. He has ardent disciples today. The propagation of His truth necessitates disciples and disciplers for the future.

Jesus Christ's earthly ministry commenced with the words "Come, follow me . . . and I will make you fishers of men" (Matt. 4:19). His earthly ministry closed with the words "Go and make disciples" (28:19). It is the duty, responsibility, and privilege of every born-again believer not only to be a disciple but also to be a discipler.

The imperative of this command demands personalized vision, crystallized objectives, and realistic methods.

This study is a result of that vision being personalized in the heart and mind of a pastor and a handful of Spirit-filled staff and laypersons. Working as a committee, these dedicated disciplers crystallized their objectives and determined that, with God's help, they would produce a simple but effective procedure that would enable them to confront their city with the claims of the gospel. They labored with prayerful seriousness as they shared the concept in small-group settings and formulated a course of study.

That which is "forever . . . settled in heaven" (Ps. 119:89, NASB) must be made available to those of us here on earth. "Go and make disciples" is a direct mandate from heaven. The prayer of the committee is that the material included in *Today's Disciple* will better enable you to fulfill this mandate and to be assured that you can fully rely on the strength and character of the One who said, "And lo, I am with you always, even to the end of the age" (Matt. 28:20, NASB).

Introduction

Saul of Tarsus was a man of great learning and eloquence. But all of his learning and all of his degrees were swallowed up by his sense of personal inadequacy when he met the Christ of the Damascus Road. Instead of requiring penance from Saul, the Lord placed upon him a mantle for which he seemed ill-suited: the commission to "go and make disciples" (Matt. 28:19).

In spite of his broad education, in spite of his training in persuasion, in spite of his enthusiasm for spreading the Good News, this man knew that he first had to take full measure of the divine-human relationship mentally and experientially before attempting to share. He perceived that he must *be* a disciple before he could "go and make disciples."

In his own words, before he ever presented himself to Peter, he said, "I went immediately into Arabia and later returned to Damascus. Then after three years, I went up to Jerusalem to get acquainted with Peter" (Gal. 1:17-18). He felt an urgent need to explore all dimensions of the Great Commission in three years of study, meditation, and prayer, and to make them an integral part of himself. He could not presume to lead others upon a path he did not know.

In this book, we attempt to explore definitively Jesus' intentions in the Great Commission. We have striven to obtain an understanding of His mandate as we have built a pyramid in which each block assists our comprehending, experiencing, and following that command in our personal lives.

Deleting pious platitudes and cutting through unrealistic clichés, we have tried to deal with the divine-human relationship in the complexities of life. We have looked at life as it is and have endeavored to demonstrate the relevance of the Word to daily issues.

Once we intellectually understand and personally experience what is involved in *being* a disciple, then we are best prepared to "go and make disciples." The last part of the book deals with specific ways and means we believe will enable us to "go out into the highways and hedges" (Luke 14:23, KJV) and "make disciples."

The purpose for this book is to prepare all of us who know Jesus Christ as personal Savior to be able to *communicate* verbally and nonverbally the Good News to everyone we meet. The prayer of the Curriculum Committee is that, with the background of this intensive study, we may have training to match the purity of our motivation, we may have knowledge to match the dimension of our enthusiasm, and we may have the expertise in discipling so we can effectively obey the Great Commission: "Go and make disciples."

For several years we have labored toward this goal. We now send forth our efforts in this volume with the prayer that those who seriously study its pages will be enabled to become powerful respondents to Christ's call to "go and make disciples."

I

Mandate
of the Master

Introduction

Summary

Go and teach, i.e., disciple, all nations, and you cannot make disciples unless you are a disciple yourself.

—*Oswald Chambers*

I

Mandate of the Master

JESUS COMMISSIONED HIS FOLLOWERS TO "MAKE DISCIPLES."

He told his disciples, "I have been given all authority in heaven and earth. Therefore go and make disciples in all the nations, baptizing them into the name of the Father and of the Son and of the Holy Spirit, and then teach these new disciples to obey all the commands I have given you; and be sure of this—that I am with you always, even to the end of the world."   *(Matt. 28:18-20, TLB)*

For this reason, it becomes the duty, responsibility, and privilege of every born-again believer not only to be a disciple but also to be a discipler.

We invite you to join us as we learn together how to fulfill the Great Commission.

I. General Purpose of This Study

Lao-tzu once said: "A journey of a thousand miles must begin with a single step." To embark on the journey of becoming a disciple involves knowing where you are beginning from, where you want to go, and how to get there from here.

How do I get there from here?

This demands honest personal evaluation. You may begin your evaluation by looking at four groups of individuals. Although it is difficult to categorize people completely, from a general point of view every person falls into one of the following categories:

> 4—Non-Christian
> 3—Uninvolved Christian
> 2—Involved Christian
> 1—Christian Discipler

When you look at these categories, there are general questions that come to mind:

> 1. Where am I now?
> 2. Where do I want to be?
> 3. How do I get there from here?

This study is designed to help you answer these questions. The purpose of this study will have been achieved:

● When your Christian life has been deepened, broadened, and enriched.

● And when, under the leadership of the Holy Spirit, you have sensed the call of God to become a discipler and have developed a lifestyle of obedience to that call.

II. Definitions Essential to This Study

A. A Christian Disciple (Follower of Christ)

A true disciple is a person who has a deep, abiding love for the person of Christ, an unshakable faith and confidence in the Word of Christ, and is committed to Christ in obedience and service.

The Bible identifies a disciple as:

● One who is totally committed to Jesus Christ. This means that every activity and every thing in your life is surrendered to Christ's Lordship (Luke 14:26-27, 33).

● One who is diligently saturating life with the Word of God through consistent Bible intake (John 8:31).

● One who is developing a devotional life by consistently experiencing a daily quiet time and a growing prayer life (Ps. 5:3; Mark 1:35).

● One whose loyalty and love, demonstrated by a servant heart, characterize a regular involvement in the fellowship of the local church (1 John 1:3; Heb. 10:24-25).

● One who demonstrates a desire to make Christ known to others by sharing regularly a personal testimony and the gospel with increasing skill (John 15:8).

B. A Discipler

A true discipler is a disciple who is consciously allowing Christ to reproduce His life, through him or her, into the lives of others.

The Bible describes the discipler as:

- One who is consistently growing in each area listed under "A Christian Disciple" (2 Pet. 3:18).

- One who is demonstrating the ability to be effective in personal evangelism by leading others to Christ (Acts 8:29-31, 37-38).

- One who has discipled another person as defined under "A Christian Disciple" (1 Thess. 2:11-13).

- One who is currently discipling others (Col. 1:28-29).

C. Christian Discipling

Discipling is reproducing in the lives of others what Christ has shown us through His Word and through the Holy Spirit. It is the process of investing oneself in the lives of others.

III. Challenge of This Study

In order to see the potential and significance of this program, the following geometric progression is offered.

If you were to train 100 people in this course of discipling for a period of one year, and these 100 people were to become disciplers, the effects would appear as in the chart on page 16.

The point is not so much that these percentages will be the actual average, but rather that when everyone does a little, the effect is startling.

Put yourself in the chart. Suppose you worked at it with 8 people in your first group, and 2 of them became disciplers. Then each of the 2 disciplers developed a group of 8 for one-year intervals. After eight years your groups would have trained 26,241 people.

There is an old saying: "By the yard it's hard, but by the inch it's a cinch." There was never a time when this saying could be truer or more thrilling than today!

It would be neither wise nor profitable to God's kingdom to get all caught up in these large figures. Instead, consider that Jesus loves all persons the same and longs for us to bring our neighbors to Him. It would please Him if you would:

- Commit yourself to study earnestly the material in this course.

- Relax about the future and be open to His leadership.

Are you secure with that approach?

In all thy ways acknowledge him, and he shall direct thy paths.

(*Prov. 3:6*, KJV)

Time in Training	Disciplers	Disciples	To Become Disciplers	Accumulative Total Lives Touched
1 year	100	800	100	900
2 years	200	1,600	200	2,500
3 years	400	3,200	400	5,700
4 years	800	6,400	800	12,100
5 years	1,600	12,800	1,600	24,900
6 years	3,200	25,600	3,200	50,500
7 years	6,400	51,200	6,400	101,700
8 years	12,800	102,400	12,800	204,100

Time in Training	Disciplers	Disciples	To Become Disciplers	Accumulative Total Lives Touched
1 year	100	800	200	900
2 years	300	2,400	600	3,300
3 years	900	7,200	1,800	10,500
4 years	2,700	21,600	5,400	32,100
5 years	8,100	64,800	16,200	96,900
6 years	24,300	194,400	48,600	291,300
7 years	72,900	583,200	145,800	874,500
8 years	218,700	1,749,600	437,400	2,624,100

Explanation: The first table is based on the fact that one disciple out of each small group of eight disciples would become a discipler. The second table is based on the fact that two disciples out of each small group of eight disciples would become disciplers.

IV. Tools of This Study

A. Syllabus

This is your guide for all that is done in discipling. Study your syllabus and bring it to class.

B. Bible

You will be using the Word in every session; therefore, bring your favorite translations. The following are all useful.

King James Version
New American Standard Bible
New International Version
New Revised Standard Version
The Living Bible

C. Marker

Consider using a colored marker and possibly a coding system to help you personalize the Word.

D. Journal

Recognizing that a daily personal devotional time is essential to the Christian walk, some have found journaling to be a useful practice.

V. Method of This Study

A medical doctor does not become a physician just by reading the book; it takes hands-on experience as well. And so it is with discipling. The group of which you are a part plays a strategic role in helping you become a disciple. The questions that are asked and the discussion that follows are as much a part of the curriculum as is the discipling manual. Through the sessions of instruction as well as in the discussion periods the goal will be to accomplish three things with any scripture or concept explored in these sessions:

A. Understand

What does this passage teach? Do I clearly understand what this passage is really teaching? Do I understand this concept?

B. Experience

Do I experience this truth in my life now? How does my life stack up when put alongside this truth?

C. Communicate

Do I know how to convey this truth? Can I explain this to others? How do I organize this to share with my family and friends?

VI. General Format of This Study

In these sessions, our time will be divided approximately in these proportions:

Discipling Curriculum Training—two-thirds of the time

Sharing, Praying, and Building Relationships—one-third of the time

VII. Specific Objectives of This Study

The specific objectives of these classes are to help you fulfill the Great Commission in your own life by following Christ and to help you invest your life in the lives of other people.

When you have completed these discipling sessions, it is our prayer that you will:

A. Be a New Testament disciple of Jesus Christ—one who is at the Master's disposal.

B. Learn to receive fresh instruction from the Spirit of God through His Word.

C. Believe that the Great Commission is for all believers.

D. Know how to disciple others and become continually involved in discipling others.

E. Discover that vitality for Christian living flows through a fourfold lifeline:
   1. Learning fresh spiritual insights and instruction
   2. Worshiping (private and public)
   3. Fellowshipping (large- and small-group)
   4. Reaching (ministry or service)

F. Recognize that quality is the key to the multiplying process in training the disciple. Multiplication is assured only when there is the proper training of people who can carry the training process into succeeding generations.

G. Understand that discipling others cannot be done solely through a classroom setting. It must also include on-the-job training, which is the imparting of one life into another.

H. Recognize that a disciple must:

    1. Know Bible doctrine (1 Pet. 3:15).

    2. Keep in daily touch with God (Acts 2:42-47).

    3. Have a strategic, effective plan for making new converts (Acts 8:4; 20:20.)

    4. Know how to use a variety of tools and methods in helping people grow spiritually.

I. Be able to evaluate your own spiritual growth and maturity.

J. Develop an awareness level of, and an active concern for, the spiritual growth and maturity of others.

Summary

Jesus calls each believer to "go and make disciples" and to teach these disciples to make disciples. Matt. 28:18-20 is indeed, for the Christian, a commission to spread the gospel. To begin the process, evaluate your beginning point, clearly discern what it is that God is calling you to be, and develop a realistic, Bible-based strategy for making God's plan a reality.

There is no substitute for the Word of God when it comes to discovering His will for our lives. "But what is the Word of God? How can I most effectively discover its truth for my life?" These and other questions will be explored in chapter 2.

2

The Word of God
in the Life
of a Disciple

Introduction

Summary

The whole Bible was given to us by inspiration from God and is useful to teach us what is true and to make us realize what is wrong in our lives; it straightens us out and helps us do what is right.   *2 Tim. 3:16, TLB*

2

The Word of God in the Life of a Disciple

When by faith you welcomed Jesus Christ into your life to be your personal Savior, you became a child of God by virtue of being born of the Spirit. As a member of the family of God, you have begun a personal relationship with Jesus Christ.

Think of it! You, creature of the dust, given breath from the Life-Giver, are a member of God's family. Imagine: *knowing* the Creator God, discovering His mind, trusting your needs to His care! What a privilege! As you develop this relationship, you will mature into your full potential in Christ.

You may immediately wonder, "How is this vital, growing relationship to be pursued? What tools are available to me, and how do I employ them?"

Two sources of strength are available to you to assure your success in reaching your full potential in Christ. They are the Word of God and the Holy Spirit.

The prophets of old were at once students of, as well as contributors to, the Scripture of their time. Ezra's method of saturating his life with the Word of God included *studying, practicing,* and *teaching* God's Word. Notice that this method corresponds with the goals of this discipling course—that is, understand, experience, and communicate.

> For Ezra had set his heart to *study* the law of the LORD, and to *practice* it, and to *teach* His statutes and ordinances in Israel.
>
> *(7:10, NASB, italics added)*

Jeremiah, too, had committed himself to filling up his life with God's Word, with this resulting heart cry:

> Thy words were found and I ate them, and Thy words became for me a joy and the delight of my heart; for I have been called by Thy name, O LORD God of hosts. *(15:16, NASB)*

As previously stated, one of the points of the profile of a disciple is "one who is diligently saturating life with the Word of God through consistent Bible intake." Hear Jesus' words as recorded by John:

> If ye continue in my word, then are ye my disciples indeed; and ye shall know the truth, and the truth shall make you free.
>
> *(8:31-32, KJV)*

One of God's choice followers, George Müller, once indicated that the position the Bible holds in your life and thoughts directly reflects the intensity of your relationship to Christ. He stated this axiom in light of his own personal experience. For the first four years following his conversion, he neglected the Word of God, resulting in his remaining a babe, both in knowledge and grace. Following these four years, he began to search diligently the Scriptures; this led to growth and blessing.

In considering these statements, you may now ask:

- What is the Word of God?
- What does it mean to saturate my life with the Word of God?
- How do I saturate my life with the Word of God?

WHAT IS THE WORD OF GOD?

An intriguing discovery is to be made in the verses below. Notice that the left-hand column contains statements from the Bible about Jesus. The right-hand column contains statements from the Bible about the Scriptures themselves and about the spoken word. An interesting equation develops as you proceed.

JESUS CHRIST	THE SCRIPTURES
The Word became flesh . . . *John 1:14* . . . and his name is the Word of God. *Rev. 19:13*	All Scripture is God-breathed. *2 Tim. 3:16*
. . . and your years will never end. *Heb. 1:12*	. . . but my words will never pass away. *Matt. 24:35*
. . . and this life is in his Son. *1 John 5:11*	The words I have spoken to you . . . are life. *John 6:63*
. . . of the Son he loves . . . all things were created by him and for him. *Col. 1:13, 16*	The universe was formed at God's command. *Heb. 11:3*
In him we have redemption through his blood . . . *Eph. 1:7*	You have been born again . . . through the . . . word of God. *1 Pet. 1:23*
He is faithful . . . will . . . purify us. *1 John 1:9*	You are already clean because of the word I have spoken to you. *John 15:3*
The Father . . . has entrusted all judgment to the Son. *John 5:22*	That very word which I spoke will condemn him at the last day. *John 12:48*

The Bible is the Word of God in a _____ ;
Jesus is the Word of God in the _____ .

CONCLUSIONS

1. Any attack against Scripture is an attack against Jesus Christ (John 5:31-40).
2. Spiritual growth requires that Jesus Christ and the written/spoken Word of God never be separated (1 Pet. 2:2-3).
3. The Word must not be used for information only (1 Thess. 1:5).
4. Any concept of Jesus apart from the Word is a false "Christ" (Matt. 24:23-24).

The Word by which God spoke the worlds into existence, the Word that has been written and has come down to us through history, and the Word that became flesh and dwelt among us are not different in character but agree perfectly.

WHAT DOES IT MEAN TO SATURATE MY LIFE WITH THE WORD OF GOD?

In studying the following diagrams, note how it is possible, in a very practical way, to saturate your life with the Word of God.

God's Word in the written or spoken form can be taken in through your *soul and spirit functions*—that is, mind, will, and emotions—by hearing, reading, studying, or memorizing.

The ultimate purpose of this saturation is for us to feel our spirit. Our spirit was created in God's own image, and it longs to have that image fulfilled. It is exciting to know that the Word itself assists us in becoming transformed into His image (2 Cor. 3:17-18). Examine two ways in which the Word assists us:

- When the Word of God, written or spoken, is accepted, it not only affects the spirit but also helps to bring the soul functions into meaning and balance.

- Even if the Word of God, written or spoken, is rejected, it still has an effect on the soul and spirit (Heb. 4:12).

Not only does God's Word enter from the external into the internal, but also Christ himself, the incarnate Living Word, living in the heart of every born-again Christian, finds expression as He lives His life through the spirit, the soul, and the body of each believer.

The Word in us lives out His life *through* us.

This is what Paul means when he states, *"Christ in your hearts is your only hope of glory"* (Col. 1:27, TLB, italics in original).

For those who are relatively new to the Bible, a brief look at the contents of the Scriptures will be given. There have been many schemes devised to assist people in their understanding of the content and general format, organization, structure, and divisions of the Bible. One such device is included here.

Three-Point Outline of the Bible
I. GOD'S INTENTION (Gen. 1 and 2) II. SIN'S INCEPTION (Gen. 3:1-13) III. GOD'S INTERVENTION (Gen. 3:14—Revelation)

Although this outline is correct, beyond the first three chapters of Genesis it gives the reader little more insight than he had before. So a second scheme is offered that will assist you in understanding the contents of the Scriptures. It is outlined on the following page.

HOW DO I SATURATE MY LIFE WITH THE WORD OF GOD?

Five means of saturating your life with the Word of God will be considered as the study continues:

> I. Hearing the Word of God
>
> II. Reading the Word of God
>
> III. Studying the Word of God
>
> IV. Memorizing the Word of God
>
> V. Meditating on the Word of God

OLD TESTAMENT (39 Books)
The Account of a Nation—Israel

Rise and Fall of the Hebrew Nation — 17 Books

PENTATEUCH (LAW)
1. Genesis
2. Exodus
3. Leviticus
4. Numbers
5. Deuteronomy

HISTORY
1. Joshua
2. Judges
3. Ruth
4. 1 Samuel
5. 2 Samuel
6. 1 Kings
7. 2 Kings
8. 1 Chronicles
9. 2 Chronicles
10. Ezra
11. Nehemiah
12. Esther

Literature of the Nation's Golden Age — 5 Books

POETRY AND WISDOM
1. Job
2. Psalms
3. Proverbs
4. Ecclesiastes
5. Song of Solomon

Literature of the Nation's Dark Age — 17 Books

PROPHETIC PERIOD

MAJOR PROPHETS
1. Isaiah
2. Jeremiah
3. Lamentations
4. Ezekiel
5. Daniel

THE TWELVE PROPHETS
1. Hosea
2. Joel
3. Amos
4. Obadiah
5. Jonah
6. Micah
7. Nahum
8. Habakkuk
9. Zephaniah
10. Haggai
11. Zechariah
12. Malachi

About 400 Years Between Testaments

CHRIST / JESUS (cross)

The Old Testament looks forward to Christ's sacrifice on the Cross.

The New Testament is based on the work Christ finished on the Cross.

NEW TESTAMENT (27 Books)
The Account of the God-man—Christ Jesus

The Story of the Man

GOSPELS — 4 Books
1. Matthew
2. Mark
3. Luke
4. John

Activities of His First-Century Church

HISTORY — 1 Book

Acts

The God-man's Teaching and Principles

EPISTLES — 21 Books

Paul's Letters
1. Romans
2. 1 Corinthians
3. 2 Corinthians
4. Galatians
5. Ephesians
6. Philippians
7. Colossians
8. 1 Thessalonians
9. 2 Thessalonians
10. 1 Timothy
11. 2 Timothy
12. Titus
13. Philemon

General Letters
1. Hebrews
2. James
3. 1 Peter
4. 2 Peter
5. 1 John
6. 2 John
7. 3 John
8. Jude

The God-man's Ultimate Universal Rule

FORECAST — 1 Book

Revelation

"All Scripture is God-breathed and is useful for teaching, rebuking, correcting and training in righteousness, so that the man of God may be thoroughly equipped for every good work" (2 Tim. 3:16-17).

Pause right now and decide—on purpose—that, as you discover these five methods, you will choose to begin practicing them or something similar to them.

I. Hearing the Word of God

God wants His people to hear His Word. Seven times in chapters 2 and 3 of Revelation the admonition is given, "Hear what the Spirit says to the churches" (2:7, 11, 17, 29; 3:6, 13, 22, NASB).

Your own appetite for the Word is stimulated as you listen to the insight and applications resulting from the study of the Word by godly pastors and teachers.

A. Six Practical Methods for Effectively Hearing God's Word

1. Be prepared to listen.
   a. Obtain sufficient rest, exercise, and nutrition.
   b. Spend some time in prayer.
   c. Ask yourself, "What do I already know about this subject?" and "What questions do I have?"
   d. Try to anticipate what you think the speaker will say.
   e. Arrive unrushed with your tools: Bible, pen, paper, and perhaps a cassette recorder.

2. Sit as close to the speaker as possible.

3. As you listen, discover the main points and illustrations.

4. You can hear at a faster rate of speed than a speaker can speak. Take advantage of this difference in speed.
   a. Think back over what has already been said.
   b. Think aside, by asking, "How can I apply this?"

5. Take notes by priority—50 percent of forgetting takes place within the first 24 hours.
   a. List the Scripture references.
   b. List the main points.
   c. List the best illustrations.
   d. List whatever else you can get.

6. Decide on one major highlight, conclusion, or application from every message you hear.

B. Assignment

> Use the form "Effectively Hearing God's Word," as found on page 35, to take notes on the next sermon, message, or cassette that you hear.

II. Reading the Word of God

In Rev. 1:3 God tells us that He will bless that person who is obedient to what he reads in the Word. James exhorts us to seek wisdom from God.

> If any of you lacks wisdom, he should ask God, who gives generously to all without finding fault, and it will be given to him.   *(1:5)*

In a seminar, Dr. Ralph Earle commented, "In the Bible wisdom is moral, practical, and spiritual, not theoretical." There is a difference between merely reading and actually studying the Word. We read the Bible in order to get an overview of God's Word. Reading should result in enjoyment and refreshment. Bible reading can be exciting and profitable if we understand its purpose and apply a few simple, practical concepts. The diagram below graphically illustrates a vital relationship between Bible reading and prayer.

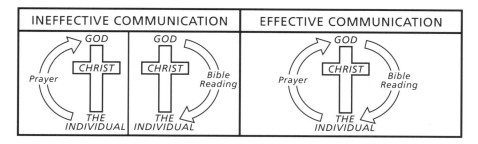

Dialogue requires two basic participants: a speaker and a listener. For effective dialogue, the roles of speaker and listener must be passed back and forth between the participants. This concept is pertinent to Bible reading (see diagram). If you resort only to letting God speak to you through Bible reading, then the dialogue is not complete. On the other hand, if you do all the talking to God through prayer without listening to His reply, there is again no dialogue. Effective dialogue occurs when you allow God to talk to you through Bible reading, and you then respond back to Him through prayer. Two helpful hints for making your Bible reading more effective for spiritual growth are described below.

A. Mark Your Bible

As you read your Bible, mark anything that impresses you. It may be a question, a conviction, or a new insight. One of the responsibilities of the Holy Spirit is to illuminate God's Word for you. Jesus said, "He will guide you into all truth" (John 16:13). After you have read a passage, go back over what you have marked, responding back to God. If you will let your response be based on what impressed you, Bible reading will take on a new dimension. Instead of a required exercise, Bible reading will become enjoyable, refreshing, exciting, and profitable!

B. Develop a Consistent Reading Plan

You may want to use the form on page 36, to keep track of where you have read in your Bible. After you read a chapter of a particular book, mark across that corresponding number on the chart. By maintaining your reading chart, you will know what you have already read and what you have left to read. Begin by reading one chapter out of the Old Testament each day as a minimum.

ASSIGNMENT

1. Begin reading and marking in your Bible.
2. Keep a record of your reading on "My Bible Reading Record," as found on page 36.
3. Share what you have read and marked in your small-group sharing time.

III. Studying the Word of God

Two New Testament letters were written to the church at Thessalonica. Upon reading each of these letters, you may be impressed with the caliber of Christians that God had raised up. However, the Berean Christians excelled the Thessalonians in one major area—Bible study.

> Now the Bereans were of more noble character than the Thessalonians, for they received the message with great eagerness and examined the Scriptures every day to see if what Paul said was true.   *(Acts 17:11)*

The study of God's Word brings you into personal discoveries of His truth. By writing down your discoveries (the distinctive characteristic of Bible study), you organize your thinking for better recall and practical application.

One simple approach to Bible study is the "Three-Point Verse Analysis."

THREE-POINT VERSE ANALYSIS

1. What does the verse say?
   After choosing a particular portion of the Bible to study, write *in your own words* what the verse says.
2. What is the context?
   Read the verses before and after the passage you are studying. Write *in your own words* the context of these verses.
3. What can be done to apply this passage?
   Write a measurable, practical, personal application.

ASSIGNMENT

Do at least one "Three-Point Verse Analysis" Bible study per week for the next four weeks. Use the form provided on page 35.

IV. Memorizing the Word of God

Probably the most effective principle leading to saturation of one's life with the Word of God is to consistently "write [it] upon the table of [one's] heart" (Prov. 3:3, KJV)—that is, memorize it! Many who have invested in consistent Scripture memorization have heartily testified that, for the investment in time and effort, Scripture memorization has returned some of the greatest dividends in their Christian lives. The psalmist recognized the value of memorizing Scripture:

> Wherewithal shall a young man cleanse his way? by taking heed thereto according to thy word. With my whole heart have I sought thee: O let me not wander from thy commandments. Thy word have I hid in mine heart, that I might not sin against thee. *(Ps. 119:9-11, KJV)*

Jesus himself had memorized Scripture, as is clearly indicated by the way He used the Word during His wilderness temptation (Matt. 4:4, 7, 10).

Scripture memorization is a skill; it can be improved. However, the key to successfully memorizing Scripture on a consistent basis is determined by the desire of one's heart. Ask yourself:

> "Do I really want to do this?"

"Does God want me to memorize His Word consistently?"

Once you are able to answer these questions with positive responses, you are ready to embark upon that most exciting path, which enables you to

> always be prepared to give an answer to everyone who asks you to give the reason for the hope that you have. *(1 Pet. 3:15)*

By applying a few simple concepts, you will soon be experiencing the thrill of hiding God's Word in your heart!

A. Begin to Memorize a Verse by:

1. Reading it through aloud several times.

2. Making a conscious effort to obtain a grasp of what the verse means—visualizing what the writer is trying to say.

3. Applying the verse to your own life in a practical way.

B. Proceed to Memorize the Verse by:

1. Asking God to help you.

2. Working on the reference and first phrase.

3. Then adding the second phrase.

4. Continuing to add phrases until you finally have the verse word-perfect.

5. Concluding with the reference again.

6. Reviewing the reference and verse several times immediately after you have completed steps 1 through 5.

7. Continuing to review the reference and verse at least once a day over the next several days.

8. Having someone check your recollection of the verse.

9. Reviewing—the only way to keep a verse sharp in your mind and ready to use.

You may have already established a different method of Scripture memorization that you feel more comfortable in using. If it works—use it!

ASSIGNMENT

Employing the principles previously given, memorize the following five verses:

Luke 9:23	Follow Christ
John 8:31	The Word
Mark 1:35	Prayer
Heb. 10:25	Fellowship
Matt. 28:18-20	Witness

Write out these verses on cards. Choose your favorite translation of the Bible. Carry these verses with you each day in your pocket or purse, and choose extra moments each day to memorize and/or review your verses. To begin, memorize at least one new verse each week.

V. Meditating on the Word of God

God expects His people to spend time—a lot of it—meditating upon His Word; this is the path that leads to blessing.

> This book of the law shall not depart out of thy mouth; but thou shalt meditate therein day and night, that thou mayest observe to do according to all that is written therein: for then thou shalt make thy way prosperous, and then thou shalt have good success. *(Josh. 1:8, KJV)*

> Blessed is the man that walketh not in the counsel of the ungodly,

nor standeth in the way of sinners, nor sitteth in the seat of the scornful. But his delight is in the law of the LORD; and in his law doth he meditate day and night.   *(Ps. 1:1-2, KJV)*

A. Results of Meditation

Meditation on what you have read is "spiritual digestion." It is the means by which you get God's Word out of the realm of mere theory into "shoe leather." It takes you from merely being a "hearer" to becoming a "doer" (James 1:22, KJV).

> Therefore everyone who *hears* these words of mine and *puts them into practice* is like a wise man who built his house on the rock.
> *(Matt. 7:24, italics added)*

The result of meditating upon God's Word is to lead you into personally applying the Word.

B. Practical Application

Without meditation and practical application, hearing, reading, studying, or even memorizing the Word of God becomes a fruitless mental exercise. Never cheat yourself or God by failing to apply the Word of God to your life in a practical, measurable manner.

> Do not merely listen to the word, and so deceive yourselves. Do what it says.   *(James 1:22)*

> But the man who looks intently into the perfect law that gives freedom, and continues to do this, not forgetting what he has heard, but doing it—he will be blessed in what he does.   *(v. 25)*

In conclusion apply the following three suggestions, which will help you make a personal application of the Word of God to your own situation.

HOW TO MAKE A PERSONAL APPLICATION FROM GOD'S WORD

1. Pray that God will give you a specific application and show you how to do it.

2. Once God speaks to you, *write out* how you fall short in that particular area. Use personal singular pronouns (I, me, etc.). Generally, your applications will be related to either your relationship with God or your relationship with people.

3. Write out specifically what God would have you do in order to correct what you wrote in number 2 above. It may take the form of memorizing a particular verse, doing a special Bible study, praying daily about the need, asking someone's forgiveness, and so on. Insure that your course of action is specific, practical, and measurable. Set time limits as required. You may want to ask someone to hold you accountable.

Summary

The relationship between God and the disciple is built through communication. This is how to come to know God: by spending time discovering who He is; by learning how He wants His children to live; and then by living according to the pattern He has given. Central to this process is the Word of God. The Word of God is packaged in a variety of forms: Jesus is the Word of God in the flesh; the Bible is the Word of God in a book; the Holy Spirit is the Living Word of God who lives in the heart of every born-again believer.

The Word of God enters your life as a believer through the means of your soul and spirit functions: that is, by hearing, reading, studying, and memorizing the Word of God. As a believer you allow the Holy Spirit to gain access to your heart. Through this means you experience the living presence of the Word of God within you.

It is important that you gain a more thorough knowledge of the Word of God. Several steps for developing greater skill in saturating one's life with the Word of God have been included in this chapter, along with more specific assignments. A duplicable form designed to foster better listening retention skills is included at the end of this chapter, along with a chart to help you record your progress in reading all the chapters of the Bible.

Central to the disciple-making process is God as revealed through His Word. You are the other person in this relationship. How are you to be viewed from a biblical perspective? How does that view correspond with current scholarship? Does God expect you to be perfect? What about sin? Chapter 3 addresses these questions. Let's turn our attention now to the focal point of God's creation—humankind.

EFFECTIVELY HEARING GOD'S WORD

Blessed is he who reads and those who hear the words of the prophecy, and heed the things which are written in it; for the time is near.   *(Rev. 1:3, NASB)*

Message Topic _____

Speaker _____ Date _____

—Scripture References—   —Miscellaneous—

—Main Points—   —Application—

—Illustrations—

Three-Point Verse Analysis

Passage_____ Date _____

Content (What does it say?):

Context (What do verses before and after say?):

Application:

Personal Application

Passage _____ Date _____ Prayed _____

Fault (Where I fall short):

Plan (What I'm going to do):

MY BIBLE READING RECORD

Old Testament

Genesis	1–50
Exodus	1–40
Leviticus	1–27
Numbers	1–36
Deuteronomy	1–34
Joshua	1–24
Judges	1–21
Ruth	1–4
1 Samuel	1–31
2 Samuel	1–24
1 Kings	1–22
2 Kings	1–25
1 Chronicles	1–29
2 Chronicles	1–36
Ezra	1–10
Nehemiah	1–13
Esther	1–10
Job	1–42
Psalms	1–150
Proverbs	1–31
Ecclesiastes	1–12
Song of Solomon	1–8
Isaiah	1–66
Jeremiah	1–52
Lamentations	1–5
Ezekiel	1–48
Daniel	1–12
Hosea	1–14
Joel	1–3
Amos	1–9
Obadiah	1
Jonah	1–4
Micah	1–7
Nahum	1–3
Habakkuk	1–3
Zephaniah	1–3
Haggai	1–2
Zechariah	1–14
Malachi	1–4

New Testament

Matthew	1–28
Mark	1–16
Luke	1–24
John	1–21
Acts	1–28
Romans	1–16
1 Corinthians	1–16
2 Corinthians	1–13
Galatians	1–6
Ephesians	1–6
Philippians	1–4
Colossians	1–4
1 Thessalonians	1–5
2 Thessalonians	1–3
1 Timothy	1–6
2 Timothy	1–4
Titus	1–3
Philemon	1
Hebrews	1–13
James	1–5
1 Peter	1–5
2 Peter	1–3
1 John	1–5
2 John	1
3 John	1
Jude	1
Revelation	1–22

"All Scripture . . . is useful . . ." (2 Timothy 3:16, NIV).

3

The Human Experience

Introduction

I. Principles to Be Understood

  A. The Historical Background

    1. The Theory of Dichotomy

    2. The Theory of Trichotomy

  B. The Modern Rediscovery of Biblical and Psychological Truth About Ourselves

  C. A Threefold Function View of Human Personality

II. Practics to Be Applied

  A. The Body Function and Characteristics

    1. The body is amoral.

    2. The body is imperfectible.

    3. The body is mortal.

  B. The Soul Function and Characteristics

    1. The soul functions are amoral.

    2. The soul functions are imperfectible.

    3. The soul functions are mortal.

  C. The Spirit or Heart Function and Characteristics

    1. The heart function is moral.

    2. The heart function is perfectible.

    3. The heart function is immortal.

  D. Some Practical Examples

    1. Physically a person needs food.

    2. Psychically a person needs to be accepted.

    3. Physically and psychically a person needs sexual relations.

  E. The Practical Aspect of the Threefold Function View As It Relates to Sin

Summary

Didst Thou not die, that I might live,
   No longer to myself but Thee?
Might *body, soul,* and *spirit* give
   To Him who gave himself for me?
Come then, my Master and my God,
Take the dear purchase of Thy blood.

          —John Wesley, italics added

3

The Human Experience

In the previous chapter, "The Word of God in the Life of a Disciple," a simple diagram was used to illustrate how God's Word can saturate your life (p. 25). In this chapter that diagram will be enlarged upon as you discover how the various aspects of human nature can function in relationship to a spiritual God and His creation. You are going to enjoy this chapter as you discover some of the basic principles regarding God's most complex creation: the human person.

Throughout this chapter you will be called upon to think carefully about the principles being presented. You will need to understand them in order to relate to such future subjects as "The Born-again Life" and "The Spirit-filled Life."

Mastering the terms listed below will enable you to gain the most from this chapter.

moral—that which deals with or is concerned with establishing principles of right and wrong as revealed by the Word of God

amoral—that which has nothing to do with establishing principles of right and wrong as revealed by the Word of God

perfectible—capable of being made perfect, in love or motive, *in this present life*

imperfectible—incapable of being made perfect, in love or motive, *in this present life*

mortal—subject to physical death, destined to die

immortal—imperishable, destined to live on, will not die

two-dimensional view—the theory that holds that man is composed of two kinds of essence (material and nonmaterial)

three-dimensional view—the theory that holds that man is composed of three kinds of essence (body, soul, spirit)

Now that these terms have been defined, ask God for a learner's attitude as you seek to discover the functional elements of the person. Remember, the Scripture states:

> The wisdom that is from above is first pure, then peaceable, gentle, and easy to be entreated, full of mercy and good fruits, without partiality, and without hypocrisy.   *(James 3:17, KJV)*

I. Principles to Be Understood

A. The Historical Background

For centuries Early Church leaders pondered and discussed the subject of human nature. Just exactly what were the elements that constituted human personality? They knew that each person has a body that is capable of carrying out physical functions, that is, breathing, running, seeing, working, and even reproducing. Yet there seems to be more than just the outside, observable flesh.

BODY

We can think; we can reason; we can remember. We can also feel pain, anger, excitement, and frustration. We have certain likes and dislikes: favorite foods, favorite colors, favorite games, and favorite people. We choose certain occupations, recreations, and lifestyles, while rejecting others. The range of our choices is often influenced by family, religious, or cultural perceptions of what is proper or ideal.

SOUL

We have all these traits, and yet there seems to be more—something deeper. There seems to be a reaching out for an identity with something or someone bigger than ourselves—a god. There are feelings of "rightness" and "wrongness" and "oughtness" that become the driving motivation for nearly all we do. Yet there are some things we do that seem to have nothing to do with rightness and wrongness—things we just do.

SPIRIT

These questions then arise: Do you feel pain with your body or your mind? Is frustration physical? Where does anger come from? Where does love come from? Does getting hungry have anything to do with morality? Are sexual impulses sinful? Why do some people have to wear glasses? How will these kinds of issues be affected in the life hereafter?

As you can see, that which constitutes human nature, and how that nature affects our behavior, posed some perplexing problems. Some of the Early Church leaders seemed to avoid the problem and gave their attention to other doctrinal issues. However, those who wrestled with this problem very decisively aligned themselves with one of two separate and distinct schools of thought.

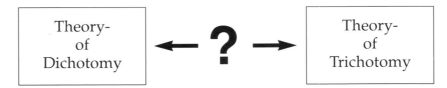

| Theory- of Dichotomy | ← ? → | Theory- of Trichotomy |

Discussion led to polarization until each of these two theories enjoyed a respectable following.

In the following pages you will have the opportunity to examine the strengths and weaknesses of each of these positions.

1. The Theory of Dichotomy

This view holds that we are made up of two kinds of essence: a material dimension (physical) and a nonmaterial dimension (spiritual). This view insists that we consist of two, and only two, distinct elements: matter and nonmatter, or material and spiritual.[1] If diagrammed, this position would be illustrated as follows.

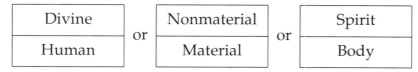

Divine		Nonmaterial		Spirit
Human	or	Material	or	Body

Some support for this two-dimensional view arises from the fact that in both the Old Testament and the New Testament the terms *soul* and *spirit* have been translated almost interchangeably. This theory provides a somewhat comfortable approach because it appears so simple and in accord with the obvious fact that we function on at least two levels: material and nonmaterial. However, there are some major limitations to the two-dimensional view.

a. It tends to break down, rather than support, the unity of the whole person.

b. It fails to stand the test when applied to practical living. As an example, it makes neither allowance for nor explanation of the difference between the moral and amoral (or morally neutral) behavior of the mind, emotions, and will.

c. It unrealistically holds that if something is not material, then it is spiritual.

Confusion has been the result whenever this theory has been applied to practical everyday living.

2. The Theory of Trichotomy

This theory suggests that humans consist of three functional elements: body (Greek, *sōma*), soul (Greek, *psychē*), and spirit (Greek, *pneuma*).[2] Wiley and Culbertson refer to the three elements as "spirit, the animal soul, and the body."[3] In *Exploring Our Christian Faith*, W. T. Purkiser states:

> This theory holds that man consists of three component parts—body, soul, and spirit—and that the soul and spirit are almost as distinct from each other as soul and body. The spirit is declared to be the organ of divine life and of communion with God, the seat of the divine indwelling. The soul is seen as the seat of the natural life, where the natural faculties of the conscious being dwell. It is the intermediary between the body and the spirit.[4]

1. H. Orton Wiley and Paul T. Culbertson, *Introduction to Christian Theology* (Kansas City: Beacon Hill Press, 1946), 153.

2. A. M. Hills, *Fundamental Christian Theology* (Pasadena, Calif.: C. J. Kinne, 1931), 1:327.

3. Wiley and Culbertson, *Introduction to Christian Theology*, 153.

4. W. T. Purkiser et al., *Exploring Our Christian Faith* (Kansas City: Beacon Hill Press, 1960), 210.

Some scriptural references may be noted that seem to lend support to this theory. It is well to remember that body, soul, and spirit are so united as to form one integrated personality.

The three-dimensional view would appear something like this:

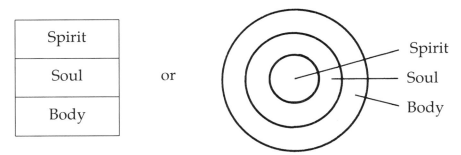

From a surface examination of this theory it looks fairly complete; yet it suffers from the same kinds of limitations found in the two-dimensional view.

a. It makes no provision for integration of the whole person but rather tends to segment the different aspects of human nature.

b. It breaks down when applied to practical living. It makes neither allowance for nor explanation of the difference between the moral and amoral (or morally neutral) behavior of the mind, emotions, and will (nonmaterial).

Not many decades ago scholars treated thinking, feeling, and choosing as almost separate faculties. Does it make any difference whether they are separated or treated as interdependent? The 19th-century theologian Dr. John Miley is quoted in the writing of A. M. Hills as having closed a discussion of these competing viewpoints of human nature by saying,

> We have reached no dogmatic conclusion on the question. Indeed, it does not seriously concern any important doctrine of Christian theology. It is a question of speculative interest in biblical psychology, but has no doctrinal implications decisive of either its truth or falsity.[5]

Doesn't it really matter, really? Is the question nothing more than a speculative one, without practical consequences?

B. The Modern Rediscovery of Biblical and Psychological Truth About Ourselves

The explosion of modern knowledge has taken some principles that once seemed obscure and unimportant and made them acutely relevant. This is especially true of our understanding of human nature and behavior.

A brief look at the history of the science of neurology might

---

5. Hills, *Fundamental Christian Theology,* 1:328.

help us better understand the need for addressing the person as a whole as well as the benefits of discussing our separate functions. The human brain is the most intricate mechanism in nature. Intensive laboratory research into the structure of the brain began in the 1920s. Early research identified the location on the brain of the control center for specific functions.

Soon a map was developed, assigning certain faculties of sense or motor skills to specific regions of the brain (sight—occipital lobe; smell—olfactory bulb; vital processes—medulla oblongata; voluntary movements and balance—cerebellum). Research has continued along this vein for decades; today, neurologists have a respectable catalog of functions—especially, sense functions and motor skills—which they are able to assign to specific locations on the brain.

However, laboratory research has generated some questions that are not easily answered. How do you account for the recurrence of a remembered event when the locus of that recorded event has been surgically removed? Is it possible that *higher mental processes* are recorded in the brain differently from simple *motor and sense responses?*

Dr. Karl Pribram, the Stanford neuropsychologist, cites the *hologram,* a three-dimensional image re-created from the patterns of laser light, as providing an adequate example to help us address this problem articulately. Stated simply, the hologram assists us in redefining perceptions: It reveals the *dimensionality* of any object photographed; it shows, concurrently, the height, width, and depth of the object. *The hologram provides a model of how the brain seems to operate in the distribution and storage of memory and other higher mental processes; the information interfaces with, or resonates throughout, a cortical network.* Its storage is not limited to a two-dimensional locus but rather penetrates into other regions of the brain as well.[6]

Pribram, called "the Magellan of brain science," has offered us a theory that leads to a *holistic view* of brain function when considering *higher mental processes.* (This in no way negates the work of researchers who have mapped out the function locus of specific motor senses, and other cognitive processes; Pribram was addressing higher mental processes.) *Giving holism its appropriate place is a trend not limited only to the field of neurological research;* it is a trend that is apparent throughout a cross section of medical disciplines today: psychiatry, psychology, general medical practice, nutrition, allergy research, and others.

Throughout the sciences dealing with human personality, the complexity of man is becoming increasingly respected. It is difficult to compartmentalize physiological operation into traditionally accepted, rigidly walled pigeonholes. The need for a *holistic approach to our functioning* is readily apparent.

---

6. Daniel Coleman, "Holographic Memory," *Psychology Today,* February 1979, 70-84.

What is true in humans physiologically is also true of our behavior. The complexity of our behavior cannot be described adequately by treating as separate, isolated faculties thinking, feeling, and choosing. Such a division is at best artificial.

Here are three reasons why it *is* important that we understand how we function as persons:

● First, psychology has progressed from being a branch of philosophy to becoming the science of behavior. Contemporary studies in psychology have assisted the Bible scholar in gaining a clearer insight into the interrelationships between thinking, feeling, and choosing. As early as 1930, Dr. Edgar P. Ellyson and Dr. H. Orton Wiley declared in a training manual for Sunday School teachers that

> the old psychology analyzed (nonmaterial) life into intellect, sensibility and will. The new psychology, in order to hold more firmly the unity of personality, has very correctly dropped this as an analysis of life. But we cannot get away from certain facts. While life is not divided into three separate parts, or independent capacities dividing the personality . . . we know that each person has and exercises all of these powers; so we can use this analysis as expressing life's functions. The unity of the personality is in no sense destroyed by this, for none of these powers function independently. *In fact, they do not function at all; they are but directions in which the person functions.* When we speak of one or more of these functions, we simply indicate the form in which the person is acting; it is the person knowing, the person feeling, or the person willing. These powers are so united in one person that each to some degree affects the other in every exercise. Each bit of knowledge produces some feeling and has a tendency to produce action; each feeling brings some knowledge and influences the will; each choice and action is known and felt *(italics added).*[7]

● Second, Bible scholars investigating the original Greek and Hebrew texts for hidden nuances of meaning have discovered an overwhelming emphasis in both the Old and New Testaments on the unity of human persons. The unity of the human person is clear from the Bible's teaching about creation. When God "formed man of the dust of the ground, and breathed into his nostrils the breath of life" (Gen. 2:7, KJV), Adam became a living person in body, soul, and spirit.

It is also clear in the biblical definition of our moral duty. Moses declared we could only keep the law of the Lord, expressed in the Ten Commandments, by practicing wholehearted allegiance to God. "Hear, O Israel: The LORD our God, the LORD is one. Love the LORD your God with all your heart and with all your soul and with all your strength" (Deut. 6:4-5). And finally, redemption in Christ aims to hallow every part of those who are saved. Paul prayed, "And the very God of peace sanctify you wholly; and I pray

---

7. Edgar P. Ellyson and H. Orton Wiley, *A Study of the Pupil* (Kansas City: Nazarene Publishing House, 1930), 32-33.

God your whole spirit and soul and body be preserved blameless unto the coming of our Lord Jesus Christ" (1 Thess. 5:23, KJV).

This Judeo-Christian understanding of the wholeness of the human person who functions as body, soul, and spirit was distorted by the influence of Greek philosophy on Christian doctrine. The Greeks insisted on an essential distinction between the material and the nonmaterial: between soul and spirit on one hand, and body on the other. That alien distinction influenced centuries of Christian thought about human nature, prompting some even to believe people could be saved in their souls (or in their spirits, if they distinguished between the two) and yet allow their bodies to behave viciously. Old Testament scholars from both liberal and evangelical backgrounds have united to call attention to the fact that we act as whole and morally accountable persons.

- Third, you and a new generation of born-again believers like you are bent on taking seriously the biblical call to glorify God with your whole self.

If you wish to become a true disciple of the Lord Jesus Christ, it does make a difference whether or not you understand your human nature and what happens to that nature when you are, first, born of the Spirit and, later, filled with the Spirit. A frequently overlooked benefit of possessing this level of spiritual understanding is that you will be able to distinguish clearly between the things in you that are *changed* and those that are *influenced* by the Holy Spirit's complete working in your life. God's Word bids you to "present your whole being" to Him, and to escape conformity to the "fleeting fashion of this world" by being "transformed in your inmost nature" (Rom. 12:1-2).[8]

C. A Threefold Function View of Human Personality

In contrast to being a fragmented bunch of parts held together by some humanistic epoxy, the human being is a unit—but a unit so complex that to adequately define how it operates escapes present scholarship. The most beneficial method of addressing your nature is to observe it from a functional point of view. By isolating the functional processes of human personality, defining the characteristics of these functions, and charting the interrelationships of those functions, a human being can be cogently described as one whole person functioning through one's

Body (physical function)

Soul (psychical function)

Spirit (spiritual function)

You operate on a moment-by-moment basis in a threefold way:

---

8. As translated and quoted by Ralph Earle, *Romans*, vol. 3 in *Word Meanings in the New Testament* (Kansas City: Beacon Hill Press of Kansas City, 1974), 213, 215-16.

physically, psychologically, and spiritually. Each of these functions has characteristics that can be compared. In so doing, you gain a better sense of what the functions are about. The functions can be compared according to their (1) morality or amorality, (2) perfectibility or imperfectibility, and (3) mortality or immortality.

For example, your body is ethically neutral; its substance and capacities are not in and of themselves sinful, though they have been, like all the rest of your being, corrupted by humankind's fall into sin. This is why John Wesley insisted again and again that "mistakes, and whatever infirmities necessarily flow from the corruptible state of the body, are noway contrary to love; nor therefore, in the Scripture sense, sin."[9]

We shall find, in the next section of this chapter, that the functional characteristics of the body and the soul are the same. Now then, if two of the three functions have the same characteristics, then, in reference to these characteristics, your nature operates in a twofold function. The apostle Paul recognized this when he spoke of the "inner man" and the "outer man" (2 Cor. 4:16, NASB). So it is—your human nature is threefold in function and twofold in characteristics. But remember that every thought and deed, every conscious response of your body, mind, and soul, involves all of you—for you are, according to both biblical and current psychological understanding, one whole person.

For our study, we will describe the one, whole person from a twofold or threefold perspective.

Look at the simple review of man:

- Unity from the perspective of Personality
- Two-dimensional from the perspective of Characteristic
- Three-dimensional from the perspective of Function

NOW LOOK AT A THREEFOLD PERSPECTIVE OF THE FUNCTIONS DIAGRAMMATICALLY:

The Word in us
lives out His life
through us.

---

9. John Wesley, "A Plain Account of Christian Perfection," in *Works*, 3rd ed. (reprint, Kansas City: Beacon Hill Press of Kansas City, 1978-79), 11:396.

II. Practices to Be Applied

In the following paragraphs you will examine the various aspects of the threefold perspective of human functions. However, it is necessary that you keep in mind the unity and integration of the total person.

A. The Body Function and Characteristics

THE BODY/PHYSICAL PERSPECTIVE	
FUNCTION	**CHARACTERISTICS**
◯	1. Amoral 2 Imperfectible 3. Mortal

> But this precious treasure . . . is held in a perishable container, that is, in our weak bodies.
> *(2 Cor. 4:7, TLB)*

1. The body is amoral. From the physical perspective a person's body is what we see. Comedian Flip Wilson's character, Geraldine, used to say, "What you see is what you get!" We give expression to our personalities through our bodies. Science analyzes the body into its many parts and functions. However, from a biblical perspective your body is the vehicle by which your psychical and spiritual functions are worked out.

They constitute the grand instrument through which God intends you to act with loving faithfulness in a world of evil. As the Bible says, "Your body is a temple of the Holy Spirit" (1 Cor. 6:19, NASB). "Let not sin . . . reign in your mortal body . . . but yield yourselves unto God, as those that are alive from the dead, and your [body] members as instruments of righteousness unto God" (Rom. 6:12-13, KJV).

2. The body is imperfectible. Some bodies appear to be "more perfectible" than others. However, until our bodies die or otherwise are exchanged for a perfect *sōma pneumatikon* (the "spiritual body" discussed in 1 Cor. 15:44), we can expect such imperfections as sickness, weakness, and fatigue. Won't it be wonderful when these imperfect, mortal bodies take on the perfection of immortality?

> For this perishable must put on the imperishable, and this mortal must put on immortality.
> *(1 Cor. 15:53, NASB)*

3. The body is mortal. It will die.

> And inasmuch as it is appointed for men to die once and after this comes judgment.
> *(Heb. 9:27, NASB)*

B. The Soul Function and Characteristics

THE SOUL/PSYCHICAL PERSPECTIVE	
FUNCTION	CHARACTERISTICS
MIND EMOTIONS WILL	1. Amoral 2. Imperfectible 3. Mortal

When we observe a person from the psychical perspective, we discover the interrelated operations of:

The mind—the capacity to think and reason;

The emotions—the capacity to experience feeling;

The will—the capacity to desire and choose.

These capacities function in relationship to each other and with the body as the vehicle of expression. The soul is the *psychical* nature of a person; the Greek word is often translated *psychē*, soul. You learned in the earlier portion of this chapter that one of the historical weaknesses of trying to explain the different aspects of human nature was the tendency to so separate and segment it as to obscure its essential unity. This was especially true of aspects of the functions of the soul.

Look again at the preceding diagram. Notice how the different soul functions overlap each other. This phenomenon can be described by a popular term taken from the fields of education, construction, and psychology: *interfacing.* Interfacing is simply where a common boundary is formed of two or more bodies of spaces. It is used here to show the interaction and interdependence of the soul functions.

Your mental functions are influenced by your emotional and volitional ones. Your desires are interlocked by your emotions and intellect. Your emotions are affected by your desires and your intellect. To think that these functions can be actually isolated in everyday life is unrealistic.

1. The soul functions are *amoral.*

a. The word *mind* refers to the capacity to think and reason. On the scale of morality there is nothing righteous nor evil about your capacity to learn that two times two equals four. There is nothing righteous nor evil about your capacity to recognize that the sun is shining. This portion of your mental capacity is amoral.

b. The word *emotion* refers to the capacity to experience feeling. It is neither righteous nor evil to be totally surprised when your friends give you an unexpected birthday party (unless you lied about your age). Being grieved when your favorite pet runs away has absolutely nothing to do with morality.

c. The word *will* refers to the capacity to desire or choose. You may desire to arise at six o'clock in the morning and set your alarm accordingly. Or, you may choose to put ketchup on your french fried potatoes at lunch. Certainly these volitional functions are neither righteous nor evil; rather, they are amoral.

d. Yet it must be noted that these functions of the soul tend to be disordered and corrupted by what theologians call "original sin." This will be discussed more fully at a later time.

2. The soul functions are *imperfectible*.

In this life the human mind will always be imperfect. You will be subject to imperfect judgment and understanding. Upon occasion the ragged edge of a frayed emotion will snag when you least expect it. And because of your imperfect human judgment, you may even make some amoral choices that are regrettable. John Wesley believed

> that there is no such perfection in this life, as implies an entire deliverance, either from ignorance, or mistake, in things not essential to salvation, or from manifold temptations, or from numberless infirmities, wherewith the corruptible body more or less presses down the soul. We cannot find any ground in Scripture to suppose, that any inhabitant of a house of clay is wholly exempt either from bodily infirmities, or from ignorance of many things; or to imagine any is incapable of mistake, or falling into divers temptations.[10]

Seventeen years later he said the same thing another way:

> "A man may be filled with pure love, and still be liable to mistake." Indeed I do not expect to be freed from actual mistakes, till this mortal puts on immortality. I believe this to be a natural consequence of the soul's dwelling in flesh and blood. For we cannot now think at all, but by the mediation of those bodily organs which have suffered equally with the rest of our frame. And hence we cannot avoid sometimes thinking wrong, till this corruptible shall have put on incorruption.
>
> But we may carry this thought farther yet. A mistake in judgment may possibly occasion a mistake in practice. . . . Yet, where every word and action springs from love, such a mistake is not properly a sin. However, it cannot bear the rigour of God's justice, but needs the atoning blood.[11]

3. The soul functions are *mortal* [The Relationship of Brain to Mind]

The functions of the mind, emotions, and will, as they are known today, will one day cease to operate as they do at the present. For now they are bound organically to our physical bodies. One day the gray cerebrum, cerebellum, and medulla that we call our brain will no

---

10. Ibid., 383.
11. Ibid., 394-95 (quoted from the Minutes of the Conference of Methodist Preachers, 1759).

longer receive stimuli or interpret and emit commands. One day the motor neurons, correlating neurons, and the dendrites of the nervous system will all die and return to dust. The psalmist declared,

> My soul cleaves to the dust.   *(Ps. 119:25, NASB)*

The Christian's power to reason, feel, and choose will then take on different characteristics, for they will spring from and be housed in an immortal and glorified being.

> Who [Christ] will transform the body of our humble state into conformity with the body of His glory, by the exertion of the power that He has even to subject all things to Himself.   *(Phil. 3:21, NASB)*

C. The Spirit or Heart Function and Characteristics

THE SPIRIT OR HEART/SPIRITUAL PERSPECTIVE	
FUNCTION	CHARACTERISTICS
(heart diagram with MIND, EMOTIONS, WILL)	1. Moral 2. Perfectible 3. Immortal

From the perspective of relationship with God, the spirit is at the center of your person. The spiritual function distinguishes humans from other animal beings. The Spirit enables you to enter relationship with God. All these functions concern moral issues—issues that are to be judged either good or evil, right or wrong.

That the human soul and spirit are not identical is proved by the fact that the Holy Spirit is able to perceive the dividing line between them.

> For the word of God is living and active and sharper than any two-edged sword, and piercing as far as the division of soul and spirit, of both joints and marrow.   *(Heb. 4:12, NASB)*

The soul and spirit are obviously distinguished in the burial and resurrection of the body.

> It is sown a natural body [*sōma psychikon* = psychical or soul].

> It is raised a spiritual body [*sōma pneumatikon* = spiritual body].
>   *(1 Cor. 15:44, NASB)*

Everyone is created with a spirit. James tells us that "the body without the spirit is dead" (2:26). The writer of Ecclesiastes tells us that when we die, our spirit will return to God who gave it.

> And the dust returns to the ground it came from, and the spirit returns to God who gave it.   *(12:7)*

We also read that when Christ came up to the place of death, He "cried out again with a loud voice, and yielded up His spirit" (Matt. 27:50, NASB). Earlier in this chapter the overlapping of mind, emotions, and will was noted. The Bible uses the word "heart" in ways that reflect all three of these capacities. As mentioned earlier, these capacities may overlap in amoral ways. However, when these capacities overlap with reference to our relationship to God, we are then dealing with the spiritual function. The Bible often uses the word "heart" for this overlap of mind, emotions, and will with a spiritual function.

1. The heart function is moral.* The heart is the moral nature of a person. It is the center or seat of the basic spiritual and moral affections of man. Gen. 8:21 states that "the intent of man's heart is evil from his youth" (NASB). In 1 Chron. 28:9 we are told that "the LORD searches all hearts, and understands every intent" (NASB). "For with the heart man believes" (Rom. 10:10, NASB).

Sin is more than just the amoral mental assent of the psyche; it springs from the depths within, from the corrupt exercise of the morally responsible functions of the mind, emotions, and will that constitute our spirit. The following are some important scriptures regarding the moral functions of the human heart or spirit.

Zech. 7:12 (NASB, italics added, throughout)—They made their *hearts* like flint so that they could not hear the law and the words.
Jer. 32:40—I will put the fear of Me in their *hearts* so that they will not turn away from Me.
Jer. 24:7—. . . for they will return to Me with their whole *heart*.
Deut. 4:29—But from there you will seek the LORD your God, and you will find Him if you search for Him with all your *heart* and all your *soul*.
Ps. 119, v. 2—. . . who seek Him with all their *heart*.
    v. 7—. . . uprightness of *heart*.
    v. 10—With all my *heart* I have sought Thee.
    v. 11—Thy word I have treasured in my *heart*. (total of 13 times in this psalm)
1 Sam. 16:7—Man looks at the outward appearance, but the LORD looks at the *heart*.
1 Kings 8:39—Thou alone dost know the *hearts*.
Luke 16:15—God knows your *hearts*.
1 Kings 11:4—When Solomon was old, his wives turned his *heart* . . . his *heart* was not wholly devoted to the LORD his God. (Also 9:4 and 15:3)
Ps. 51:10—Create in me a clean *heart* . . . renew a steadfast *spirit within*.
Ezek. 11:19—I shall give them one *heart*, and shall put a new *spirit* within them.
Phil. 4:7—. . . guard your *hearts*.
Rom. 2:5—. . . stubbornness and unrepentant *heart*.
Rom. 8:27—He who searches the *hearts* knows.
Luke 24:25—O foolish men and slow of *heart* to believe.
Jer. 17:9—The *heart* is more deceitful than all else.

---

*Moral and spiritual, though not identical in meaning, are used interchangeably in this study.

Matt. 15:8—Their *heart* is far away from Me.
Matt. 19:8—Because of your hardness of *heart* . . .

One of the classic scriptures that deals with the morality of the heart function is found in Proverbs.

> Keep thy heart with all diligence; for out of it are the issues of life.
> *(Prov. 4:23, KJV)*

Please note the diagram on page 50. You will observe that all of the functions of the soul, that is, mind, emotions, and will, are present and active in the heart. This is the interfacing center of human personhood.

> The capacity of the heart or spirit includes the functions of the mind, emotions, and will in regard to moral matters—those dealing with "rightness" and "wrongness" and "oughtness."

It is true that all amoral or morally neutral exercises have nothing to do with righteousness or evil. However, some other functions of the mind have everything to do with morality. Certain *emotional* expressions are not tied to morality, while others are essentially moral. As we observed earlier, some desires or *choices* simply have to do with amoral or morally neutral decisions. However, certain choices deal with issues that are totally moral.

The heart is the citadel or moral control room of your person. There, either Christ or your selfish and sinful will is in command. The domination of either Christ or self-will over your spiritual nature will determine your moral behavior, whether observable or unobservable. With this in mind, go back and review the scriptures on the previous pages. You can then see more clearly the moral character of the heart or spirit function that you have been studying.

2. The heart function is perfectible. An entire chapter, titled "The Spirit-filled Life," will be devoted to this subject later. However, let it be stated at this point that when Christ commanded, "Therefore you are to be perfect, as your heavenly Father is perfect" (Matt. 5:48, NASB), He was not talking about a "someday," "if," or "maybe" situation. The good news is that in the spirit or heart—matters dealing with *moral intent*—there is the promise of purity based on the purity of Jesus Christ living His life through you via the Holy Spirit.

> God is love. . . . If we love one another, God abides in us, and His love is *perfected* in us. By this we know that we abide in Him and He in us, because He has given us of His Spirit. . . . God is love, and the one who abides in love abides in God, and God abides in him. By this, love is *perfected* with us, that we may have confidence in the day of judgment; because *as He is, so also are we in this world.*   *(1 John 4:8, 12-13, 16-17, NASB, italics added)*

3. The heart function is immortal. This is the part of your nature that will last eternally. How it will be "rehoused" is not known. But it is known that your spirit or heart will live on forever and forever.

D. Some Practical Examples

How does all of this apply to you in your everyday living? How will this new insight help you to live a more victorious Christian life this next week?

Before we look at some practical applications of these truths, a quick review is needed.

Below is a diagram of the threefold function perspective. This represents the whole or integrated person. Without looking back to the previous pages, label the three different functions as indicated by the arrows:

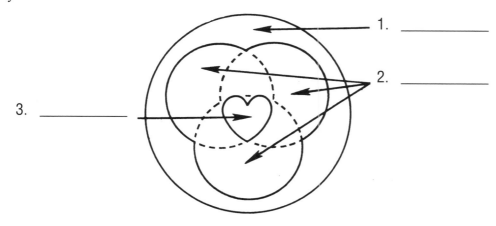

1. _____

2. _____

3. _____

Now, fill in the three characteristics for each function:

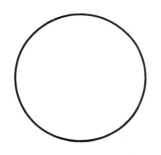

1. _____
   (Function)

CHARACTERISTICS

1. _____
2. _____
3. _____

a. _____   b. _____

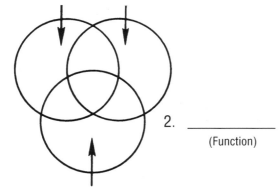

2. _____
   (Function)

CHARACTERISTICS

1. _____
2. _____
3. _____

c. _____

Notes

3. _____
   (Function)

CHARACTERISTICS

1. _____
2. _____
3. _____

Out of a possible 18 points, what was your score?

| |
| SCORE |

NOTE: During the review you may have made an interesting discovery. All of the capacities of the soul (mind, emotions, will) are also present and active in the heart. This function of the heart or spirit includes the capacities of the mind, emotions, and will in regard to moral matters—those dealing with "right" and "wrong."

If you were to diagram this fact in regard to your *mind,* it would look like this:

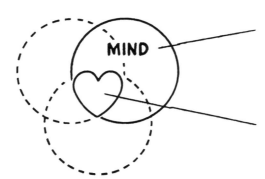

There are some activities of the mind that are amoral and have *nothing* to do with *"right"* and *"wrong."*

—HOWEVER—

There are *some* activities of the mind that are moral and have *everything* to do with *"right"* and *"wrong."*

Can you think of some examples of each?

If you were to diagram this fact in regard to your *emotions,* it would look like this:

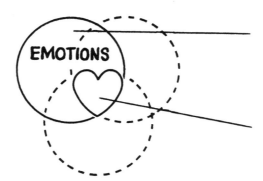

There are some functions of the emotions that are amoral and are not tied to *"right"* and *"wrong."*

—HOWEVER—

There are certain emotions that are *moral and deal with "right" and "wrong."*

Can you think of some examples of each?

If you were to diagram this fact in regard to your *will*, it would look like this:

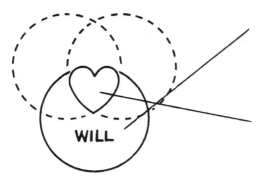

There are *some desires* or *choices* that simply have to do with *amoral issues and are not "right" or "wrong."*

—HOWEVER—

There are certain volitional choices that are totally *moral and deal with "right" and "wrong."*

Can you think of some examples of each?

The moral aspect of the heart is different from the amoral aspect of the soul, even though all three capacities—that is, mind, emotions, and will—are present and active in both.

God created us in His own image and in His own likeness (Gen. 1:26; 5:1; 9:6). It is God who is Spirit, manifesting himself through His Word, either written, declared, or living. It is He who must be the governing principle of morality in your heart. John Fletcher and Charles G. Finney thought the central promise of Scripture was in the words of the prophet Ezekiel.

> A new heart also will I give you, and a new spirit will I put within you. . . . And I will put my spirit within you, and cause you to walk in my statutes. *(Ezek. 36:26-27, KJV)*

That God himself is able to write His laws upon your heart is a fact that is impossible to fully understand or describe—but that is exactly what happens.

Consider now some practical examples of how these principles work in your everyday life:

1. Physically a person needs food. There is nothing evil about the necessity to satisfy the pangs of hunger. This is a God-given safeguard against starvation.

Suppose you go into your favorite supermarket to pick up a sandwich from the delicatessen. You are absolutely famished from the vigorous activities of the morning—and now it is lunchtime, time to eat. With that delicious sandwich in hand, piled high with meat, cheese, tomatoes, and lettuce, you head toward the checkout stand. Your mouth begins to water; you can hardly wait to bite into that sandwich. However, as you approach the checkout stand, you discover that your money is still on your dresser at home. "No problem," you say. Moments later you actually smile at the person at the checkout stand as you and your unpaid-for sandwich go out the door.

a. Was it justifiable to take the sandwich, since the total price was not over $5?

b. Is hunger moral or amoral?

c. Was this a moral issue?

d. At what point did the situation change from amoral to moral?

    (1) When you decided to eat a cheap sandwich instead of a balanced meal?

    (2) When you chose the sandwich with meat, cheese, tomatoes, and lettuce?

    (3) When you decided in your heart to take the sandwich without proper compensation?

    (4) When you smiled at the person as you went out the door?

    (5) Other?

Look again at Heb. 4:12 (NASB):

> For the word of God is living and active and sharper than any two-edged sword, and piercing as far as the division of soul and spirit.

The deciding factor that always divides the amoral soul function from the moral spirit or heart function is the Word of God revealed to us.

God said, "You shall not steal" (Exod. 20:15, NASB). There is absolutely nothing evil about the need for food. There is absolutely nothing evil about the choice to eat or even of what to eat. However, when you decided in your heart to take something that was not yours—and, without rendering the required compensation, made it yours—then you faced a moral choice, a decision of the heart. Moral issues are always centered around the point of choice (volitional or willful act). The rightness or wrongness of the choice is determined by the Word of God, either written or alive.

2. Psychically a person needs to be accepted. There is nothing inherently evil about the need to be accepted. Suppose you and several of your friends are having coffee at a local restaurant, discussing generalities. The name of a common acquaintance comes up in the discussion. You feel insecure and threatened by the very mention of this person. Because of your insecurity you employ subtle "leveling" devices to elevate yourself and demean the other person.

Here are two of the most common ways:

a. by innuendo, that is, raising an eyebrow, shrugging the shoulders, and so on; or

b. by telling something about this person that may be true but should not be told.

Everybody laughs, and you feel accepted.

Has this amoral psychical need to be accepted become a moral issue? The answer is no. As stated previously, there is nothing inherently evil about the need to be accepted. However, it is a moral issue when, in the heart, you choose to deceive, exaggerate, or harm another in order to be accepted.

This is true in your sales record, your golf score, or any other way you choose to exaggerate.

Is it, then, a moral issue to drive a car or live in a house you can't afford in order to impress someone and gain acceptance?

3. Physically and psychically a person needs sexual relations. Certainly there is nothing inherently evil about God's plan to equip you with a sex drive.

Suppose you were Joseph, number 11 son of Jacob. Joseph was hundreds of miles away from home. No one really knew Joseph's situation, and certainly, what with his having been sold as a slave by his own family, it would appear as though no one really cared. No one, that is—except Potiphar's wife. With every imaginable method of seduction, she tried to persuade Joseph to choose evil. But Joseph realized that there was more to be considered than the satisfaction of a physical or psychical need (Gen. 39).

> For the word of God is living and active and sharper than any two-edged sword, and piercing as far as the division of soul and spirit.
> *(Heb. 4:12, NASB)*

Even though the Ten Commandments had not been given yet, it was the living, active Word of God that enabled Joseph to choose righteousness in this situation of moral choice. When does the amoral sex drive become a moral issue? It becomes a moral issue whenever it moves outside the sanctity of marriage. Fornication (premarital sex), adultery (extramarital sex), and homosexuality are three examples of sexual activity outside the sanctity of marriage. But the sex *drive*, in and of itself, is amoral. The point of determination is God's Word and our volitional response to its instruction.

> You shall not commit adultery.   *(Exod. 20:14, NASB)*

In the Sermon on the Mount, Jesus carried the thought even further by emphasizing the fact that the morality of the situation *precedes* the actual physical act.

> You have heard that it was said, "YOU SHALL NOT COMMIT ADULTERY"; but I say to you, that everyone who looks on a woman to lust for her has committed adultery with her already in his heart.
> *(Matt. 5:27-28, NASB)*

Jesus is not declaring that the amoral sex drive or curiosity is evil. He is saying that when you decide in your heart that, if given the opportunity, you would respond to the physical and psychical drive outside the parameters of marriage, you have already committed adultery in your heart.

James, the brother of Jesus, likewise dealt with this issue:

> But each one is tempted when he is carried away and enticed by his own lust [natural desire]. Then when lust [natural desire] has conceived, it gives birth to sin; and when sin is accomplished, it brings forth death.   *(1:14-15, NASB)*

It is the choice or intent of the heart that gives any situation morality.

E. The Practical Aspect of the Threefold Function View As It Relates to Sin

Drawing a clear-cut distinction between the *amoral* functions of the body and soul and the *moral* function of the heart will help you to become, with the help of the Holy Spirit, all that God has in mind for you to become.

Historically, many have defined *sin* as "any deviation from absolute perfection, whether known or unknown, voluntary or involuntary."

This definition fails to make clear a distinction between the *amoral* body and soul functions and the *moral* function of the heart. Under this definition, one is forced to concede that every amoral thing human beings do is "sin," because ideally it could be better. Thus it falls short of an absolute standard of perfection.

The weaknesses of this legal definition are readily apparent. Dr. H. Orton Wiley quotes John Wesley: "Calling that sin which is not sin, opens the door also to actual sinning."[12]

Dr. Purkiser states:

> But to make everything sin is, in effect, to make nothing sin. It is impossible to grade sins. *If forgotten promises, faulty judgment, and human limitations and infirmities are sins, then there is no qualitative distinction possible between such so-called sins on the one hand and lying, theft, or immorality on the other.* The door then is left open wide to sin of all sorts *(italics added).*[13]

Dr. Metz adds:

> First, a wrong concept of sin may make preaching a path to hypocrisy, an avenue to despair, or a road to presumption. Preaching may lead to hypocrisy when it tends to make sin exclusively legal or objective. Such preaching tends to encourage Pharisaism, for it ignores the inner area of motive and desire. Preaching may lead to despair when it makes that sin which is not sin and the sensitive soul lives under a continual cloud of condemnation. Preaching may lead to presumption when sin is committed freely and continually because of false notions about the inability of divine power to free one from those moral and spiritual aberrations which need to be eliminated.[14]

---

12. H. Orton Wiley, *Christian Theology* (Kansas City: Beacon Hill Press, 1940-43), 2:508.
13. Purkiser, *Exploring Our Christian Faith*, 307.
14. Donald Metz, *Studies in Biblical Holiness* (Kansas City: Beacon Hill Press of Kansas City, 1971), 72.

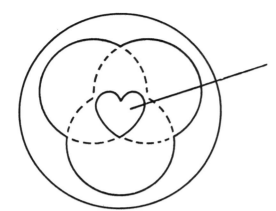

The heart is the function that deals with moral issues. It is the perfection area that deals with motive and intent. It is the moral function of the mind, emotions, and will that has the capacity to choose righteousness or evil.

The term *sin*, as used to describe human conduct in the New Testament, *always implies conscious choice.* The idea that sin is a conscious and moral act of the will is consistent with the entire teaching of the New Testament.

> There is therefore now no condemnation to them which are in Christ Jesus, who walk not after the flesh [the old sinful nature], but after the Spirit. *(Rom. 8:1, KJV)*

> No one who lives in him [Christ] keeps on sinning. . . . Dear children, do not let anyone lead you astray. He who does what is right is righteous, just as he [Christ] is righteous. He who does what is sinful is of the devil, because the devil has been sinning from the beginning. The reason the Son of God appeared was to destroy the devil's work. No one who is born of God will continue to sin. *(1 John 3:6-9)*

These scriptures become meaningless if "sin" is to include all the imperfections and deviations from absolute perfection, whether known or unknown, voluntary or involuntary, that characterize the morally neutral activities of our souls and bodies.

John Wesley's concise and consistent summation of the New Testament teaching of sin is difficult to improve upon:

> Sin . . . a voluntary transgression of a known law.[15]

> The Christian consciousness and conscience recognize that there *is* a significant qualitative difference between mistakes, errors, and lapses on one side and voluntary transgressions of divine law on the other. When judged by the law of *objective right,* there is no difference between a forgotten promise and a broken promise. When judged by the law of *objective right,* there is no difference between a misstatement of fact made in ignorance and a lie. In each case, something promised has not been performed and an untruth has been stated.

> But there is a tremendous difference in these two types of sit-

---

15. Wesley, "Plain Account," 396.

uations subjectively and ethically. In the case of both forgotten promise and ignorant misstatement, *there is regret—but not guilt. There is sorrow but not sin.* Lapses of memory and ignorance are always deplorable and should be avoided as far as possible. But the Christian consciousness does not find in these infirmities anything which would interrupt its fellowship with God or bring to it condemnation and a sense of guilt.

. . . *Sin is fundamentally a matter of choice, of intention, and of purpose (italics added).*[16]

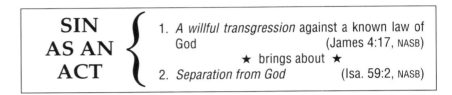

The problem of sin is twofold. The following diagram illustrates this principle:

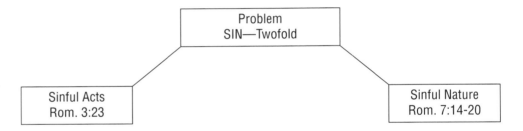

Summary

The present chapter has dealt with two main themes: the complexity of human nature and how sin affects that nature. Human personality is an integrated unit; we cannot physically separate personality from the body; nor can we physically reduce the body into elements of soul and spirit. However, distinctions of body, soul, and spirit can be made when looking at how human personality *functions.* This is called the threefold function view.

This threefold function view describes what we believe is a biblical model of human nature. By stressing the need to view our functional parts within the context of a unified, integrated person, the biblical model appears to be remarkably consistent with a holistic approach to human personality as expressed throughout a variety of scientific disciplines.

16. Purkiser, *Exploring Our Christian Faith*, 307-8.

In this discussion of human nature, the following assumptions have been made: (1) human personality is an integrated whole; (2) the components into which human behavior can be divided at a functional level have been identified; (3) the interrelationship of these components to each other and their impact on the whole person has been described. Upon closer examination, human behavior emanates from functions that are characterized as follows:

Function	_Characteristics_
Body	Amoral, imperfectible, mortal
Soul	Amoral, imperfectible, mortal
Spirit	Moral, perfectible, immortal

The key characteristic with which we have dealt is morality. A legitimate concern that we might voice is, "How can you know when an issue is a moral issue versus when it is an amoral issue?" Heb. 4:12 tells us that the Word of God is uniquely empowered to reveal the morality of an issue to the human heart.

> For the word of God is living and active and sharper than any two-edged sword, and piercing as far as the division of soul and spirit. (NASB)

An underassessed spiritual hazard awaits those who have not adopted a scriptural definition of *sin*. Several scholars have forecast some dangers that accompany a misconception of sin:

> Dr. Purkiser: "To make everything sin is . . . to make nothing sin."

> Dr. Wiley: "Calling that sin which is not . . . opens the door to actual sinning."

In the New Testament sin always implies conscious choice. John Wesley has crafted a definition of *sin* that is clearly consistent with New Testament teaching:

> Sin . . . a voluntary transgression of a known law.

Expounding upon this view, Purkiser says that "sin is fundamentally a matter of choice, of intention, and of purpose."

Throughout this Discipling Curriculum, sin is considered as an act *and* a corrupted condition of the heart's moral capacities of the mind, emotions, and will.

The following two chapters will deal with the acts of sin (chap. 4), the nature of sin (chap. 5), and the remedy for each.

4

Born-again Life

Introduction

Summary

Redemption in His blood
   He calls you to receive;
"Come unto Me, the pard'ning God.
   Believe," He cries, "believe!"
                    —*John Wesley*

4

The Born-again Life

In this chapter, we will deal specifically with basic biblical teachings about the born-again life.

You cannot, of course, understand your own nature fully from a simple diagram. There is no way to adequately describe through graphics or charts the complexity of the individual. However, as you saw in chapter 3, the person can best be understood from a threefold function perspective. We are whole persons functioning at three levels. Understanding the three kinds of human functioning will help you understand the born-again life as God has planned.

Please begin, then, by reviewing the ways human beings function as presented in the previous chapter. In the space below draw and label the diagram of the threefold function view:

List the characteristics of each function in the boxes provided.

CHARACTERISTICS

Body	Soul	Spirit
1.	1.	1.
2.	2.	2.
3.	3.	3.

In regard to sin, fill in the box below.

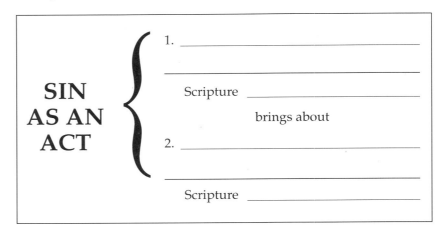

Now that we have reviewed the threefold function view and the definition of *sin* as an act, consider the following diagram, which illustrates the twofold aspect of sin and the solution for sin as an act.

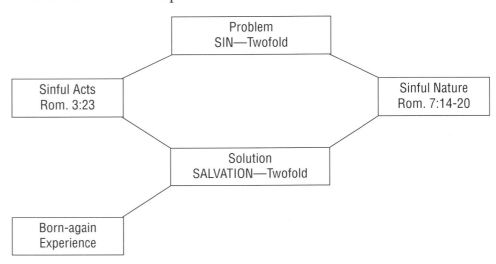

Chapter 5, "The Spirit-filled Life," focuses on the power of the Holy Spirit to help us live in a renewed relationship to God, His Word, and His will for our lives. The present chapter concerns sinful acts, their impact upon our lives, and the solution God has provided for each of us.

There are three divisions in this chapter that describe the experience of being born again and the life of Christian victory that it brings.

I. The Crisis of Being Born Again

II. The Continuation of the Born-again Life

III. The Inner Conflict in the Born-again Life

I. The Crisis of Being Born Again

The word *crisis* in this study is defined as: a turning point in human life; a time when you change direction; a moment when you choose one lifestyle over another.

The crisis through which you enter into the born-again life begins the moment the Holy Spirit convicts you. You can no longer carry the guilt nor endure the bondage of your sins; you decide to repent and trust in Christ to save you from them. In that decisive moment of separation from sin, the Holy Spirit breathes into you the new life that flows from the risen Christ; you are born anew spiritually. The crisis, then, is a life-changing, direction-turning encounter with the Holy Spirit resulting in your being born again.

How does it happen?

A. Crisis Commences with Response

The participants in this crisis are God and you as an individual—God responding to you; you responding to God. The following four steps describe the process:

- Divine Initiative
- Awareness of Need
- Awareness of Choice
- Your Response

1. Divine Initiative—God reaching out to you

God reaches out to you through the good news of Christ's redemption conveyed by means of the ever-active presence of the Holy Spirit in the world. He does not desire that you should remain separated from Him but, rather, that you should be reconciled to Him in love. Sin separates us from God; salvation (being born again) brings reconciliation.

> Whoever does not love does not know God, because God is love. This is how God showed his love among us: He sent his one and only Son into the world that we might live through him. This is love: not that we loved God, but that he loved us and sent his Son as an atoning sacrifice for our sins. *(1 John 4:8-10)*

> God so loved the world that he gave his one and only Son, that whoever believes in him shall not perish but have eternal life. *(John 3:16)*

God initiated the plan of salvation through the shed blood and sacrifice of Jesus Christ.

> God commendeth his love toward us, in that, while we were yet sinners, Christ died for us. *(Rom. 5:8, KJV)*

> God was reconciling the world to himself in Christ, not counting men's sins against them. And he has committed to us the message of reconciliation. *(2 Cor. 5:19)*

God also takes the initiative in making that plan become a reality in your heart. He does not wait for you to make the first move; instead He reaches down in an act of love with the purpose of reconciliation and redemption.

2. Awareness of Need—Recognizing your sinful condition and your need for divine forgiveness

It is the work of the Holy Spirit, who helps to bring you to the awareness of your needy condition. It is the Holy Spirit who helps you know the difference between *mistake* and *sin* by the use of either sorrow or guilt. The sinner must first be convinced that he is a sinner. There is no hope for you as long as you presume that you are all right.

> And He [the Holy Spirit], when He comes, will convict the world concerning sin, and righteousness, and judgment.   *(John 16:8, NASB)*

In convincing you of your sin, the Holy Spirit always works in conjunction with the Word of God, either written, declared, or living.

a. Written Word—The Holy Spirit dealing with you through the printed page, that is, either Scripture or written material based upon God's Word.

> List an example of the way the Holy Spirit has helped you become aware of your need through the *written* Word.
>
> _____
>
> _____
>
> _____

b. Declared Word—The word of the Holy Spirit through the proclaimed Word. This proclamation may be made by a preacher, prophet, teacher—or simply shared by a friend. The proclaimed Word is not limited to the spoken Word but also includes the declaration by example.

> List an example of the way the Holy Spirit has helped you become aware of your need through the *declared* Word.
>
> _____
>
> _____
>
> _____

c. Living Word (Christ in you)—A very powerful means that the Holy Spirit uses to make you aware of your need. You were created in the image of God, and the Holy Spirit works through that image, however tarnished it may be.

> List an example of the way the Holy Spirit has helped you become aware of your need through the *living* Word.
>
> _____
>
> _____
>
> _____

Conviction is the word most often used to describe the way the Holy Spirit makes you aware of your guilt. The Holy Spirit uses the written, declared, or Living Word to convict you of your guilt.

Sometimes the vehicle through which the Spirit works is called *conscience*. Conscience is not always uniform, but it is universal. John Wesley called this "the remains of the image of God" in fallen humanity and believed it was "found, at least in some small degree, in every child of man."

3. Awareness of Choice—Realizing your spiritual and moral responsibility

The Holy Spirit not only convicts you of your sin but also convinces you of the merits of righteousness and the surety of judgment.

> When he [the Holy Spirit] comes, he will *convict* the world of guilt in regard to *sin* and *righteousness* and *judgment*. *(John 16:8, italics added)*

Simply to convict you of sin, yet provide no deliverance from it, would be to leave you in confusion and despair. Not only does the Holy Spirit show you "a better way," a way of righteousness, but also He is faithful to convince you that if you do not break from sin, you must face judgment. This brings you to a point of having to make a decision: you are faced with a choice either to continue in sin or to seek righteousness. You are presently and finally responsible for this moral choice. The complete work of the Holy Spirit in conviction is *both* to convince you of guilt in regard to sin, righteousness, and judgment *and* to show you that you must choose one of the two alternatives. Many would like God to make this choice for them, but to do so would deny the freedom and moral responsibility He gave us. The power to choose is your noblest capacity; it is the expression of your freedom, the hallmark of your humanity, the mechanism that makes love possible. And yet it is a sobering thought that for the exercise of this power, you are eternally accountable. How you respond to your moral choice will affect you here and in the hereafter.

4. Your Response—Reacting to your spiritual and moral responsibility. Your response is either rejection or repentance.

You may choose to reject God's plan of salvation and remain in your lost condition. Your other choice is to repent.

> Repent, for the kingdom of heaven is near. *(Matt. 3:2)*

> But unless you repent, you too will all perish. *(Luke 13:3)*

Repentance not only means turning from sin but also includes a brokenness of spirit.

> It is a broken spirit you want—remorse and penitence. A broken and a contrite heart, O God, you will not ignore. *(Ps. 51:17, TLB)*

It also includes the confessing and forsaking of sins and trusting in Christ as Redeemer.

> If we confess our sins, he is faithful and just and will forgive us our sins and purify us from all unrighteousness.   *(1 John 1:9)*

> I tell you the truth, whoever hears my word and believes him who sent me has eternal life and will not be condemned; he has crossed over from death to life.   *(John 5:24)*

Forsaking of sins carries with it the thought of restitution. You must turn your back on sin and also seek to make right the wrongs you have committed—with the help and guidance of the Holy Spirit.

When you study what the Bible says about repentance, you will see it always involves turning away from conscious and willful transgressions.

> But if the wicked *turns from* his wickedness and does what's fair and just, he shall live.   *(Ezek. 33:19, TLB, italics added)*

> Then if my people will humble themselves and pray, and search for me, and *turn from* their wicked ways, I will hear them from heaven and forgive their sins and heal their land.
>   *(2 Chron. 7:14, TLB, italics added)*

> Bear fruits that are . . . consistent with your repentance—[that is,] conduct worthy of a heart changed and abhorring sin.   *(Luke 3:8, AMP.)*

Not only does repentance carry with it the idea of turning from our acts of sin, but also it includes the necessity of trusting Christ alone.

> For God's way of making us right with himself depends on faith—counting on Christ alone.   *(Phil. 3:9, TLB)*

> This righteousness from God comes through faith in Jesus Christ to all who believe.   *(Rom. 3:22)*

Without turning back in your material, please fill in the four areas of response in the space provided.

Areas of Response Regarding the Crisis of the
Born-again Life

1. _____

2. _____

3. _____

4. _____

B. Crisis Culminates in a Born-again Experience

The terms *saved* and *converted* are, many times, used interchangeably with the phrase "born again" to describe what happens when you turn from sin and trust Christ as your Redeemer.

When you as a sinner (1) respond to divine initiative, (2) become aware of your sinful condition of separation, (3) become aware that you are responsible to choose either evil or righteousness, and (4) repent—turn and trust—then something happens on the divine side. At that moment, Jesus Christ becomes for you "the Lamb of God, who takes away the sin of the world!" (John 1:29). As you turn over to Him your sins, you receive in return forgiveness, justification, regeneration, and adoption. A brief discussion of these follows.

1. Forgiveness. To the reality of this born-again experience the Holy Spirit bears witness with your spirit, giving assurance that you now possess life that is eternal, the life "in Christ."

God's forgiveness is the pardon or "remission of sins" (KJV) that frees us from the penalty and the guilt of sin. An ancient meaning of the word translated *forgive* is "to take away." The angel told Joseph of Nazareth that he should name Mary's divine Son Jesus, or Joshua, "for he shall *save his people from their sins*" (Matt. 1:21, KJV, italics added).

> If we confess our sins, he is faithful and just and will *forgive us our sins* and purify us from all unrighteousness.   *(1 John 1:9, italics added)*

> All the prophets testify about him that everyone who believes in him receives *forgiveness of sins* through his name.
> *(Acts 10:43, italics added)*

> Let the wicked forsake his way and the evil man his thoughts. Let him turn to the LORD, and he will have mercy on him, and to our God, for *he will freely pardon.*   *(Isa. 55:7, italics added)*

2. Justification. Justification is God's legal act of satisfying the demands of the Law. The ceremonial Law of Moses had required a blood sacrifice in place of the death the people merited by committing sins. Jesus Christ, having been put to death on the Cross, became that Blood Sacrifice for all who will believe on Him, in all times and places. His atonement (Lev. 5:10, NASB) allows us to be fully justified. An easy way to remember justification is that you are *"just as if"* you had never sinned."

> But now a righteousness from God, apart from law, has been made known, to which the Law and the Prophets testify. This righteousness from God comes through faith in Jesus Christ to all who believe. There is no difference, for all have sinned and fall short of the glory of God, and are justified freely by his grace through the redemption that came by Christ Jesus. God presented him as a sacrifice of atonement, through faith in his blood. He did this to demonstrate his justice.   *(Rom. 3:21-25)*

> But now he has reconciled you by Christ's physical body through death to present you holy in his sight, without blemish and free from accusation.   *(Col. 1:22)*

> Look up the following scriptures and write them out in the blanks provided.
>
> Acts 13:38-39 _____
>
> _____
>
> _____
>
> _____
>
> Titus 3:7 _____
>
> _____
>
> _____
>
> _____

Our forgiveness and justification are possible only by God's grace. He met all of the requirements of His holy law by providing the sinless Son of God as the Atoning Sacrifice for our sins, enabling us to become children of God. In the New Testament, justification is the act of God that declares *legally* this new relationship, while forgiveness establishes *experientially* that relationship. By trusting in Christ and Him alone, we are accepted and restored to God's favor.

3. Regeneration/Initial Sanctification. Regeneration is the work of the Holy Spirit that gives new life through Christ to the person who was dead in sins and trespasses. Sin results in spiritual death. Death means separation. Regeneration literally means "to live again." Therefore, *regeneration begins your restoration back to the image of God.*

> You are already clean because of the word I have spoken to you. . . . *I am the vine; you are the branches.*   *(John 15:3, 5, italics added)*

Paul taught the early believers the doctrine of regeneration using such phrases as:

> Therefore, if anyone is in Christ, he is a *new creation; the old has gone, the new has come!*   *(2 Cor. 5:17, italics added)*

> He saved us, not on the basis of deeds which we have done in righteousness, but according to His mercy, by the washing of regeneration and renewing by the Holy Spirit.   *(Titus 3:5, NASB)*

The Scriptures describe being born of God as a vast and mighty change. Look at the power of these phrases: a change "from darkness to light"; a change "from the power of Satan unto God"; a "passing from death unto life"; a "resurrection from the dead."[1]

> You were dead in your transgressions and sins. . . . But because of his great love for us, *God,* who is rich in mercy, *made us alive with Christ*

---

1. John Wesley, "The Witness of the Spirit," in *Works,* 5:118-19.

even when we were dead in transgressions—it is by grace you have been
saved. And God raised us up with Christ.   *(Eph. 2:1, 4-6, italics added)*

Notes   73

4. Adoption. Adoption is the act of God declaring that the believer,
being justified by faith in Jesus Christ, is now received into the family of God and given all the privileges of His family.

> Those who are led by the Spirit of God are sons of God. For you
> did not receive a spirit that makes you a slave again to fear, but you
> received the Spirit of sonship. And by him we cry, *"Abba,* Father."[2] The
> Spirit himself testifies with our spirit that *we are God's children.* Now if
> we are children, then we are heirs—heirs of God and co-heirs with
> Christ.   *(Rom. 8:14-17, second italics added)*

Adoption occurs at the same moment as forgiveness, justification, and regeneration; but in the order of thought it logically follows them. And sometimes the witness of the Spirit to our adoption actually does follow afterward.

In Scripture the witness of the Spirit is variously called the assurance, the knowledge, or the testimony that "God has given us eternal life, and this life is in his Son" (1 John 5:11). John Wesley declared that the promise of the witness of the Spirit was "one grand part of the testimony" that God gave to the early Methodists "to bear to all mankind."[3] Referring to Rom. 8:16 ("The Spirit himself testifies with our spirit that we are God's children"), Wesley made it clear that the preeminent witness is God's Spirit.

> The testimony of the Spirit is an inward impression on the soul,
> whereby the Spirit of God directly witnesses to my spirit, that I am a
> child of God; that Jesus Christ hath loved me, and given himself for
> me; and that all my sins are blotted out, and I, even I, am reconciled to
> God. . . . This testimony of the Spirit of God must needs, in the very
> nature of things, be antecedent to the testimony of our own spirit . . .
> even the testimony of our own conscience, that God hath given us to
> be holy of heart, and holy in outward conversation. It is a consciousness of our having received, in and by the Spirit of adoption, the tempers mentioned in the word of God, as belonging to his adopted children; even a loving heart toward God, and toward all mankind.[4]

Assurance is the product of the interaction between two parties: the Spirit of God and the spirit of the believer.

> *Those who obey* his commands *live in him,* and *he in them.* And this
> is how we know that he lives in us: We *know* it by *the Spirit he gave us.*
>   *(1 John 3:24, italics added)*

> Dear friends, let us love one another, for love comes from God.
> *Everyone who loves has been born of God and knows God.* Whoever does
> not love does not know God, because God is love.   *(4:7-8, italics added)*

---

2. The word *Abba* is the untranslated Aramaic word used in Palestine in Jesus' time
meaning "Father," but conveying a closer sense of intimacy and identity than our sometimes formal use of "Father."

3. John Wesley, "The Witness of the Spirit, Discourse II," in *Works,* 5:124.

4. John Wesley, "The Witness of the Spirit, Discourse I," in *Works,* 5:115.

> 1. FORGIVENESS gives pardon from the guilt and penalty of sin.
> 2. JUSTIFICATION gives fulfillment of the demands of the Law.
> 3. REGENERATION gives new life through Christ.
> 4. ADOPTION gives reception into the family of God.

Your born-again relationship does not in any way destroy your power to choose. Once your relationship with the Lord begins, you do not switch onto "automatic pilot." The condition of the born-again person is secure only so long as he or she chooses to remain an adopted child. If you subsequently choose to commit a sin (a willful transgression against the known law of God), you are once again separated from God.

However, if you who are born again choose to "walk in the light, as he [God] is in the light," then you have fellowship with God, "and the blood of Jesus, his Son, purifies us from all sin" (1 John 1:7). Your condition is then secure, and no external force can move you from that security; nothing can except *your* own choice. Rom. 8:14 states, "Those who are led by the Spirit of God are sons of God." Consequently, the born-again person can say with Paul:

> For I am convinced that neither death nor life, neither angels nor demons, neither the present nor the future, nor any powers, neither height nor depth, nor anything else in all creation, will be able to separate us from the love of God that is in Christ Jesus our Lord. *(vv. 38-39)*

No wonder John Wesley's favorite sermon text in the early years of his ministry was the good news of "holiness and happiness" found in Rom. 14:17:[5]

> The kingdom of God is not a matter of eating and drinking, but of righteousness, peace and joy in the Holy Spirit.

In the space provided below, list and give a brief explanation of the four responses included in the crisis of the born-again life.

	Response	Explanation
1.	_____	_____
2.	_____	_____
3.	_____	_____
4.	_____	_____

---

5. John Wesley, "The Way to the Kingdom," in *Works,* 5:77-81.

List below and give a brief explanation of the four results of the born-again crisis.

	Result	Explanation
1.	_____	_____
2.	_____	_____
3.	_____	_____
4.	_____	_____

Now let's continue the development of our theological diagram by adding to the problem of sin as an act, its solution.

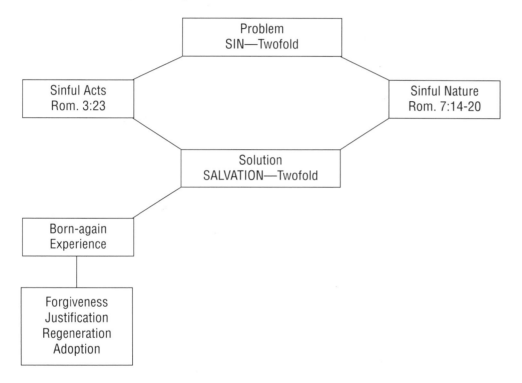

Problem
SIN—Twofold

Sinful Acts
Rom. 3:23

Sinful Nature
Rom. 7:14-20

Solution
SALVATION—Twofold

Born-again
Experience

Forgiveness
Justification
Regeneration
Adoption

II. The Continuation of the Born-again Life

What happens in the interim between the crisis of the new birth and the Spirit-filled life? For a certainty, you will be faced with spiritual conflict and moral confrontations as you continue in the born-again experience.

Theologically, the distinction between the words *confrontation* and *conflict* is:

> CONFRONTATION—the act of facing, or being presented with, moral alternatives

> CONFLICT—a fight, clash, or struggle for moral mastery

As a new Christian, make every effort to discover your spiritual potential for handling impending problems successfully. Adjustments must be made. Alterations in lifestyle may be proven necessary. You must discipline yourself in order to grow. Your internal adjustments will lead to spiritual conquests that will be externalized in observable behavior.

Consider the internal adjustment needed for the successful continuation of the born-again life.

A. Internal Adjustments Necessary to This Continuation

There are a number of simple commitments to new attitudes that will help establish you as a new Christian and keep you from falling away. Paul instructs the church in Colossae to adopt these same attitudes.

1. Steadfastness is the key to conquest. Your decision for Christ must be reinforced by a continuing determination to be victorious.

> Once you were alienated from God and were enemies in your minds because of your evil behavior. But now he has reconciled you by Christ's physical body through death to present you holy in his sight, without blemish and free from accusation—if you continue in your faith, *established and firm, not moved from the hope* held out in the gospel. *(Col. 1:21-23, italics added)*

2. The attitude of **thankfulness,** when counting your blessings in times of discouragement, will bring God's presence very near. Growth in gratitude will develop your power of praise.

> So then, just as you received Christ Jesus as Lord, continue to live in him, rooted and built up in him, strengthened in the faith as you were taught, and *overflowing with thankfulness.*
> *(Col. 2:6-7, italics added)*

3. Reverence and godly fear will produce, under the guidance of the Holy Spirit, a desire for immediate and constant obedience.

> When you were dead in your sins and in the uncircumcision of your sinful nature, God made you alive with Christ. He forgave us all our sins, having canceled the written code, with its regulations, that was against us and that stood opposed to us; he took it away, nailing it to the cross. *(Col. 2:13-14)*

4. Your spirit will show the open-mindedness of the **"learner's heart."** Your heart will be filled with a burning desire to take advantage of every God-given opportunity to advance, to progress, and to grow.

> Since, then, you have been raised with Christ, *set your hearts on things above,* where Christ is seated at the right hand of God. *Set your minds on things above,* not on earthly things. *(Col. 3:1-2, italics added)*

5. With the help of God, develop an attitude of **self-discipline,** and determine to change any undesirable patterns of physical or mental habit that hinder your new way of life. This may require a reassessment of your ambitions, life purposes, and goals.

> *Put to death,* therefore, whatever belongs to your earthly [also, sinful, TLB] nature: sexual immorality, impurity, lust, evil desires and greed, which is idolatry. Because of these, the wrath of God is coming. You used to walk in these ways, in the life you once lived. But now you must *rid yourselves* of all such things as these: anger, rage, malice, slander, and filthy language from your lips. Do not lie to each other, since you have taken off your old self with its practices and have put on the new self, which is being renewed in knowledge in the image of its Creator. *(Col. 3:5-10, italics added)*

6. Your attitude of **forgiveness,** reflecting the grace in which God has forgiven you, will protect you from the pitfalls of resentment, injured feelings, and a bitter or critical spirit toward others.

> Therefore, as God's chosen people, holy and dearly loved, clothe yourselves with compassion, kindness, humility, gentleness and patience. Bear with each other and *forgive* whatever grievances you may have against one another. *Forgive as the Lord forgave you.* And over all these virtues *put on love,* which binds them all together in perfect unity. *(Col. 3:12-14, italics added)*

7. The testimony or **witness** of your Christian experience will strengthen your own faith. It may bring inspiration or conviction to the lives of others.

> Let the word of Christ dwell in you richly *as you teach and admonish one another* with all wisdom, and *as you sing psalms,* hymns and spiritual songs with gratitude in your hearts to God. *(Col. 3:16, italics added)*

8. Be an **optimistic** Christian, with your optimism arising from fully invested faith in God's faithfulness.

> Whatever you do, *work at it with all your heart,* as working for the Lord, not for men, since you know that you will receive an inheritance from the Lord as a reward. *It is the Lord Christ you are serving.* *(Col. 3:23-24, italics added)*

9. The attitude of **faithfulness** in your prayer life will solve problems, salvage situations, and build an inner strength for continued growth.

> Is any one of you in trouble? He should pray. Is anyone happy? Let him sing songs of praise. Is any one of you sick? He should call the elders of the church to pray over him and anoint him with oil in the name of the Lord. And *the prayer offered in faith* will make the sick person well; the Lord will raise him up. If he has sinned, he will be forgiven. Therefore confess your sins to each other and pray for each other so that you may be healed. *The prayer of a righteous man is powerful and effective.* *(James 5:13-16, italics added)*

Your daily devotional reading of Scripture will reveal other needs for attitudinal adjustment that will help you achieve victorious continuation of the born-again life. Now let's direct our attention to some external adjustments that will result from your new internal attitudes.

B. External Adjustments Necessary to This Continuation

External adjustments are those observable changes that result from your attitudinal adjustments.

1. An adjustment to **regular church attendance** will be necessary if you are not already in the habit of attending. You will find yourself enjoying the influence and inspiration of fellow Christians; these relationships will replace old, sinful associations. The church is composed of the believers and is part of the Body of Christ. It is the family of God. It is where Christians find strength and encouragement. Maturity takes place best within the environment and spiritual influence of the church.

2. Adjustments must be made to **cultivate new friendships** and associations that are in harmony with your new ideals and concerns. Your new direction as a born-again Christian will tend to separate you from the fellowship of those who are truly adverse to your newfound faith. However, there will be others in your circle of influence who notice the change in your life, and from among them new converts will be won.

3. An adjustment will be made in **responding to human needs** whenever a hurt or need appears. An attitude of awareness to human need will enable you to see the suffering and hear the hurts of those around you. You will become God's hands and feet to touch the lives of those in need.

In the following blanks, list and briefly describe the external adjustments you believe are necessary in each of the areas as they apply to you.

4. Recreation _____

_____

_____

_____

_____

5. Physical Habits _____

_____

_____

_____

_____

6. Stewardship:

a. Time _____

_____

_____

_____

b. Money _____

_____

_____

_____

c. Talent _____

_____

_____

_____

7. Other _____

_____

_____

8. Other _____

_____

_____

A variety of such internal and external adjustments must be made in your new life. Making these adjustments as you continue to follow God's plan for your life is a maturing process indeed. Therefore, *these adjustments need to be purposely nurtured, carefully cultivated, and zealously guarded.* They must be maintained in spite of all opposition.

> Then said Jesus to those Jews which believed on him, If ye continue in my word, then are ye my disciples indeed; and ye shall know the truth, and the truth shall make you free.   *(John 8:31-32, KJV)*

> "We must go through many hardships to enter the kingdom of God," they said.   *(Acts 14:22)*

You will not always succeed, especially in the early days of your Christian life. And though you need not fail at any point, you may on occasion do so and be tempted to despair. Remember, then, what the aged apostle John wrote to the early Christians:

> My dear children, I write this to you so that you will not sin. *But if anybody does sin,* we have one who speaks to the Father in our defense— Jesus Christ, the Righteous One. He is the atoning sacrifice for our sins, and not only for ours but also for the sins of the whole world. We know that we have come to know him if we obey his commands. . . . Whoever claims to live in him must walk as Jesus did. *(1 John 2:1-3, 6, italics added)*

III. The Inner Conflict in the Born-again Life

Review the experience of the born-again life, using the diagram below.

Born-again Life

CRISIS	CONTINUATION
1. Divine Initiative	
2. Awareness of Need	
3. Awareness of Moral Choice	
4. Your Response	CONFLICT

Confrontation and Temptation—Confrontation and Temptation

1. Forgiveness
2. Justification
3. Regeneration
4. Adoption

You have looked at the crisis of the born-again life; you have also considered the continuation of the born-again life; and you have noted the necessity for positive adjustments in attitude as a result of the internal and external confrontations of this new life. As you proceed, a conflict is sure to arise, for there is a struggle for moral mastery in the heart of every born-again believer. Examine now the basic cause for this conflict.

A. Original Sin Is the Basis for Inner Conflict

John Wesley often quoted the ninth article of faith of the Church of England, which declared, "Original sin is the corruption of the nature of every man, whereby man is in his own nature inclined to evil, so that the flesh lusteth contrary to the Spirit."

Indeed, Wesley noted "this grand point" that "the flesh, evil nature, opposes the Spirit, even in believers . . . through all the Epistles of St. Paul, yea, through all the Holy Scriptures."[6]

Paul described the *origin* of this infection of our moral natures:

> Sin entered the world through one man, and death through sin, and in this way death came to all men, because all sinned—for before the law was given, sin was in the world. . . . Death reigned from the time of Adam to the time of Moses, even over those who did not sin by breaking a command. *(Rom. 5:12-14)*

---

6. John Wesley, "Sin in Believers," in *Works*, 5:145, 147.

But he rejoiced in Christ's promise of *deliverance* from it:

> If, by the trespass of the one man, death reigned through that one man, how much more will those who receive God's abundant provision of grace and of the gift of righteousness reign in life through the one man, Jesus Christ.   *(Rom. 5:17)*

1. What, then, is the inward effect of the remains of this evil nature in your life as one who is born of the Spirit? Original sin, which is often referred to as inherited depravity or *inbred sin, is an infection of the moral nature of fallen humanity.* It is the ever-present tendency toward self-will and rebellion against the purpose and will of God.

Of course, no person—not even the most sinful unbeliever—is totally evil or without any trace of inward goodness; but human depravity is "total" in the sense that this bent toward sinning affects all the functions of your body, soul, and spirit.

From the moment you are born again, you no longer suffer "condemnation," for you "walk not according to the flesh but according to the Spirit" (Rom. 8:1, 4, NRSV). *But your present victory over the power of inbred sin is threatened by the continued presence of this inner inclination to yield to temptation.*

This remaining impurity of your heart inhibits God-given desires and appetites and distorts the functioning of your mind, emotions, and will. Until this inward pollution is cleansed away through your being filled with the Holy Spirit, every confrontation with moral choice will generate some degree of inner conflict. There are many different terms used by theologians (or found in the Scriptures) that describe the nature and effects of original sin.

inbred sin	sin in the flesh
indwelling sin	depraved nature
inward pollution	propensity to sin
enmity against God	root of bitterness
carnality	the old Adam
the old man	the sin in believers
the sin principle	war against the Spirit
the law of sin	uncleanness
bent toward sinning	fallen nature
the carnal mind	rebellion
double-mindedness	impure heart
infection of the moral nature	

2. Original sin in your heart as a born-again believer manifests itself by prompting you to choose alternatives contrary to the will of God.

Without God, your human nature is set upon its own way rather than the way of God. It expresses itself in enmity against God's Lordship over your life. The remains of indwelling sin in the believer's heart often cause great inner conflict. The fleshly nature, the virus of sin that is rooted deep in your heart, spreads its effects over every function of your body, soul, and spirit.

B. Diagrams of the Three Conditions of the Human Heart

The three possible conditions of the heart may be illustrated by the diagrams above. Although there is no way to diagram adequately the human heart or spirit, these will help you understand it from a functional point of view.

 The self-centered heart illustrates the sinner with self on the throne, whose life is controlled by original sin and is plagued by accumulated acts of sin. Self is on the throne and God is left outside the heart.

> Those who live according to the flesh set their minds on the things of the flesh. . . . Those who are in the flesh cannot please God. *(Rom. 8:5, 8, NRSV)*

 The conflicted heart illustrates the born-again life into which the Spirit of Christ has come to reside; however, the fleshly nature with its bent toward sinning is still present. The persistence of inner strife results. The coexistence of the new life in Christ and the deep remains of corruption in the heart *create conflict* in the heart and affect all the capacities of the soul—mind, emotions, and will. The bent toward sinning finds its way, all too often, into the conscious attitudes and actions of born-again believers.

> The moment we truly believe in Christ . . . we are not then renewed, cleansed, purified altogether; but the flesh, the evil nature, still *remains* (though subdued) and wars against the Spirit. So much the more let us use all diligence in "fighting the good fight of faith." So much the more earnestly let us "watch and pray" against the enemy within. *(John Wesley)*[7]

7. Ibid., 156.

I have been crucified with Christ and I no longer live, but Christ lives in me. The life I live in the body, I live by faith in the Son of God, who loved me and gave himself for me.   *(Gal. 2:20)*

 The God-enthroned heart represents the entirely sanctified or cleansed heart. This is the heart in which Christ lives and from which all original sin has been cleansed, making it possible for God to control and direct such a life.

For in Christ all the fullness of the Deity lives in bodily form, and you have been given fullness in Christ, who is the head over every power and authority.   *(Col. 2:9-10)*

Summary

In this present chapter we have discovered that, while we have been greatly impacted by sin, God has not left us hopeless. Rather, through Christ's atoning blood He has opened a way for all who will to come to Him. His Word instructs us: "Ye must be born again" (John 3:7, KJV).

The process by which one is born of the Spirit is set in motion by God's divine initiative: He has reached out to all with forgiving love. He has established redemption through the gift of His Son on the Cross. His work of redeeming grace has been complete. Yet it does not work in our behalf until we, by faith, receive His offer of forgiveness; we are given the privilege of exchanging our sin for His Son.

When by faith we trust in Him, He forgives, justifies, regenerates, and adopts us into His family.

As we continue in the born-again life, some noticeable changes become apparent. New attitudes are spawned within us: steadfastness, thankfulness, reverence for God, a "learner's heart," self-discipline, forgiveness, a desire to witness, optimism, and faithfulness. These are changes that we can see within ourselves. Changes that others can see include attending church regularly, cultivating friendships that are compatible with our new ideals, and finding ways to respond to human needs around us.

One development that frequently catches by surprise us who are new believers is the conflict we begin to experience as we continue in the born-again life. Things were seemingly going well, when all of a sudden we are overwhelmed by the awareness of a struggle for moral mastery within.

We should not be dismayed by this occurrence. Just as it is a surprise for each believer, so was it a surprise for the Early Church fathers. "How is it that Christians sin? Are we never to be released from sin's grasp?" The question of the presence of sin in the life of the born-again believer is a question that has hounded such theologians as Augustine, John Calvin, James Arminius, and others. We will address this problem and the scriptural answer to it in chapter 5.

5

The Spirit-filled Life

Introduction

I. The Crisis of the Spirit-filled Life

    A. The Spirit-filled Life Commences with a Response

        1. Divine Initiative

        2. Awareness of Need

        3. Awareness of Choice

        4. Your Response

            a. Acknowledge

            b. Confess

            c. Commit

            d. Believe

    B. The Spirit-filled Crisis Culminates in a Sanctified Experience

        1. Heart Purity

        2. Heart Perfection

            a. The heart of every Spirit-filled Christian reflects the love of God.

            b. Human motives stem from inner drives.

        3. The Infilling of the Holy Spirit

        4. The Empowering of the Holy Spirit

II. The Continuation of the Spirit-filled Life

    A. Growth

        1. A More Intense Love for His Word

        2. A More Intense Love for Others

        3. An Eager Adjustment to New Light Revealed

        4. Influence and Effect on the Amoral Functions

    B. Confrontation and Temptation but No Conflict

        1. Confrontation

        2. Temptation

        3. No Conflict

III. The Concerns Regarding the Spirit-filled Life

Summary

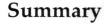

The sanctifying Spirit pour,
  To quench my thirst and wash me clean.
Now, Saviour, let the gracious shower
  Descend, and make me pure from sin.
—Charles Wesley

written in 1741 to accompany John Wesley's
first sermon titled "Christian Perfection"

5

The Spirit-filled Life

The Spirit-filled life, like the born-again life, is described in different ways in the Bible. Those who in our day testify to this experience frequently employ the following terms:

> Christian perfection (Matt. 5:48)
> entire sanctification (1 Thess. 5:23, NASB)
> Christian holiness (Rom. 6:22)
> perfect love (1 John 4:16-18)
> renewal in the divine image (2 Cor. 3:18, KJV)
> heart purity (Acts 15:9)
> fullness of the blessing (Rom. 15:29, KJV)

The Spirit-filled life begins when believers in Christ are filled with the Holy Spirit (Acts 1:5 and 2:4; Eph. 5:18).

This experience may well be defined as

> that act of God, subsequent to regeneration, by which believers are made free from original sin, or depravity, and brought into a state of entire devotement to God, and the holy obedience of love made perfect.
>
> It is wrought by the baptism with the Holy Spirit, and comprehends in one experience the cleansing of the heart from sin and the abiding, indwelling presence of the Holy Spirit, empowering the believer for life and service.
>
> Entire sanctification is provided by the blood of Jesus, is wrought instantaneously by faith, preceded by entire consecration; and to this work and state of grace the Holy Spirit bears witness.[1]

Oswald Chambers, a well-known devotional writer of the 20th century, wrote:

> Salvation means that we are brought to the place where we are able to receive something from God in the authority of Jesus Christ, viz., remission of sins.

---

1. *Manual*, 1993-97, Church of the Nazarene (Kansas City: Nazarene Publishing House, 1993), 30-31, par. 13.

Then there follows the second mighty work of grace—"and inheritance among them which are sanctified." In sanctification the regenerated soul deliberately gives up his right to himself to Jesus Christ, and identifies himself entirely with God's interest in other men.[2]

J. A. Wood quotes the German United Brethren Church as saying:

By perfect holiness we understand the separation and purification from all inhering sin, after regeneration, by the blood of Jesus Christ, the Son of God; and the filling of the heart with the love of God by the Holy Ghost."[3]

He also states:

Charles Wesley put it into his hymns, and without caviling over it, millions have sung for a century:

"Give us, Lord, this second rest."
"Speak the second time, be clean."
"Let me gain that second rest."

Even the Calvinistic Augustus Toplady wrote:
Let the water and the blood,
From Thy wounded side which flowed,
Be of sin the double cure,
Save from wrath, and make me pure.[4]

Our theological diagram below illustrates the twofold aspect of our salvation.

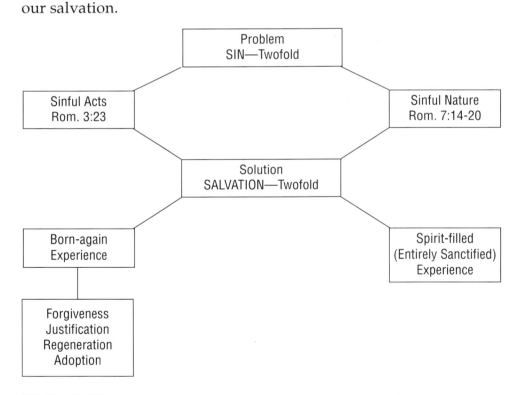

_____

2. Oswald Chambers, *My Utmost for His Highest* (New York: Dodd, Mead, and Co., 1965), 10.

3. J. A. Wood, abridged by John Paul, *Perfect Love* (Kansas City: Beacon Hill Press, 1954), 20-21.

4. Ibid., 94.

I. The Crisis of the Spirit-filled Life

A. The Spirit-filled Life Commences with a Response

Look again at the diagram that was partially presented on page 80. The diagram takes you to the point of Conflict. This state of conflict develops as a result of your identifying with both the positive and negative alternatives with which you have been confronted. A spirit of rebellion surfaces. This is moral conflict.

The crisis of the Spirit-filled life includes the following four areas of response:

- Divine Initiative
- Awareness of Need
- Awareness of Moral Choice
- Your Response

1. Divine Initiative—God reaching out to deliver you from indwelling sin.

> No one can come to me unless the Father who sent me draws him, and I will raise him up at the last day.   *(John 6:44)*

> And so Jesus also suffered outside the city gate to make the people holy through his own blood.   *(Heb. 13:12)*

God continues to reach out to you by means of the ever active presence of the Holy Spirit in the heart of the believer. God, in His holiness, cannot look with favor on the inward pollution of the uncleansed heart, even though it is the heart of a believer. God longs to deliver His adopted children from the dilemma of their inner conflict. He does not want anything to separate them in the least degree from the intimacy of His fellowship and favor so that perfect conformity to His divine will may be experienced in their lives.

Through the Atonement, He has initiated a twofold plan of salvation that effectively remedies the divided allegiance of the double-minded condition.

> God made him who had no sin to be sin for us, so that *in him we might become the righteousness of God.*   *(2 Cor. 5:21, italics added)*

> For what the law was powerless to do in that it was weakened by the sinful nature, God did by sending his own Son in the likeness of sinful man to be a sin offering. And so *he condemned sin in sinful man, in order that the righteous requirements of the law might be fully met in us, who do not live according to the sinful nature but according to the Spirit.*
> *(Rom. 8:3-4, italics added)*

2. Awareness of Need—You recognize your deeper spiritual need. The acute awareness of moral conflict will lead you to a sense of your own desperate need for divine assistance. The apostle Paul graphically portrays this desperate need:

> What a wretched man I am! Who will rescue me from this body of death?   *(Rom. 7:24)*

The Holy Spirit brings you to the awareness of your need and enlivens your heart with the hope that there is a solution for your conflict. Just as He worked in you awakening your conscience to the need for forgiveness, so the Spirit works through the Word, drawing, illuminating, and convicting you of the need to be sanctified.

The time has come to admit to yourself and to God the inner conflict you experience with the mind of the flesh and its debilitating fruit: double-mindedness.

The Holy Spirit will help you see how the condition of your divided heart has caused you to fall short of the perfect will of God. You begin to realize that your influence and example have not measured up to your own expectations—nor God's. This sense of loss will produce, under God, a great hungering and thirsting, a desperate longing and searching, for a higher spiritual level of deliverance and victorious living.

> Blessed are they which do hunger and thirst after righteousness: for they shall be filled. *(Matt. 5:6, KJV)*

3. Awareness of Choice—The recognition of your responsibility to seek deliverance from indwelling sin. The Holy Spirit throws the searchlight of revealed truth into your heart so that you can see clearly the ugly nature of this inner pollution, which was inherited through the Fall. This brings the alternatives into focus: choosing to continue in a state of inner conflict, or, through the experience of heart purity, experiencing the solution. You are brought face-to-face with the necessity of moral choice.

> Oh, that you would choose life; that you and your children might live! Choose to love the Lord your God and to obey him and to cling to him, for he is your life and the length of your days. *(Deut. 30:19-20, TLB)*

The power of choice, the exercise of free moral agency, is an awesome responsibility. The stakes are high. The consequences are eternal. You can choose either to have your life controlled by the fleshly spirit or by the Holy Spirit. You can choose your own selfish way, or you can choose "The Holy Highway."

> And a main road will go through that once-deserted land; it will be named "The Holy Highway." No evil-hearted men may walk upon it. God will walk there with you; even the most stupid cannot miss the way. *(Isa. 35:8, TLB)*

We must die to sin.

> So you must consider yourselves dead to sin and alive to God in Christ Jesus. *(Rom. 6:11, NRSV)*

> I have been crucified with Christ and I no longer live, but Christ lives in me. The life I live in the body, I live by faith in the Son of God, who loved me and gave himself for me. *(Gal. 2:20)*

There must be a dying out to self and to sin. This choice may be more difficult for some than others, but the sooner you let go of all perverted self-centeredness, the sooner you will receive complete deliverance. You must choose all that God has for you.

> But just as he who called you is holy, so be holy in all you do; for it is written: "Be holy, because I am holy." *(1 Pet. 1:15-16)*

BY WAY OF REVIEW FILL IN THE FOLLOWING BOXES, WHICH SHOULD ESTABLISH CLEARLY WHAT YOUR INNER NEED IS.

Define Original Sin

List Other Descriptive Terms for Original Sin

Recall an Example of What Helped You Become Aware of Your *Need* for the Spirit-filled Life. List Three.

4. Your Response—Personal reaction to your need to be sanctified and Spirit-filled. You have the alternative to either accept or reject the provisions of the Spirit-filled life. If you choose to accept the Spirit-filled life, you will need to take the following steps:

a. Acknowledge, through the help of the Holy Spirit, the extent of your need as it has been shown to you. (The basic cause of your moral conflict was the inherited, depraved nature.)

b. Confess this need to God. You are not responsible for having inherited this plague of moral infection, but you are responsible to avail yourself of God's cleansing cure.

A marvelous opportunity is set before you: Recognizing the depth of your need, you can respond in obedience to all you know of the will of God for your life.

c. Commit all you have, are, or ever expect to be. At this time, lay down your arms of inner rebellion and self-serving, and make a complete commitment and a full consecration of all of self to God.

I beseech you therefore, brethren, by the mercies of God, that ye *present your bodies a living sacrifice,* holy, acceptable unto God, which is your reasonable service.   *(Rom. 12:1, KJV, italics added)*

> In the Space Provided Describe Your Present Level of Commitment

d. Believe God to accept you and to cleanse you from all indwelling sin. Come to the point of total commitment and full consecration. Trust God with *all* of your life.

> "We are saved from sin, we are made holy, by faith." This I testified in private, in public, in print; and God confirmed it by a thousand witnesses.[5]

Wesley declares that the experience of heart purity is attained by faith.

> Exactly as we are justified by faith, so we are sanctified by faith. Faith is the condition, and the only condition, of sanctification (the cleansed and Spirit-filled life), exactly as it is of justification.[6]

You are now ready—by faith and faith alone—to step out on the unfailing promises of God. Trust that—instantly—He accepts your commitment, cleanses your heart, and fills it with the presence and power of His Holy Spirit. Here rest your case in the full assurance of the unfailing dependability of God.

> List the Areas of People's Response in Receiving the Spirit-filled Life.
> 1. _____
> 2. _____
> 3. _____
> 4. _____

B. The Spirit-filled Crisis Culminates in a Sanctified Experience

You observed in the previous section how the Spirit-filled crisis involved two responses: God to us and us to God: (1) God's response—divine initiative; (2) our awareness of our need; (3) the necessity of a moral choice; and (4) how we respond in consecration,

---

5. Wesley, *Works,* 12:368.
6. John Wesley, *Sermons* (New York: Lane and Scott, 1852), 1:388.

dedication, and faith. Upon our response, God performs the following works within our heart:

- Heart purity, or the cleansing of the heart.
- Heart perfection, which means to restore to its original purity.
- Infilling of the Holy Spirit is His uncontested indwelling.
- Empowering of the Holy Spirit is the divine energizing that comes in the absence of moral conflict.

1. Heart Purity. To purify or cleanse is to make free from adulterating matter, impurities, pollution, or corruption. The Greek word *katharidzō* means "to cleanse or purify" and is the word Peter used in referring to what happened on the Day of Pentecost. *Purify* and *cleanse* will be used interchangeably to mean "the purging of the moral nature from the carnal corruption of original sin or depravity."

Notice the emphasis God places on cleansing as He speaks through His Word:

> God, who knows the heart, showed that he accepted them by giving the Holy Spirit to them, just as he did to us. He made no distinction between us and them, for he purified their hearts by faith.
> *(Acts 15:8-9)*

> Cleanse your hands, ye sinners; and purify your hearts, ye double minded.   *(James 4:8, KJV)*

> And the very God of peace sanctify [cleanse] you wholly; and I pray God your whole spirit and soul and body be preserved blameless unto the coming of our Lord Jesus Christ. Faithful is he that calleth you, who also will do it.   *(1 Thess. 5:23-24, KJV)*

The Spirit-filled life enables us to live free *from* sin, not free *in* sin. To be cleansed from *all original sin* is a beautiful experience.

> But if we walk in the light, as he is in the light, we have fellowship one with another, and the blood of Jesus Christ his Son cleanseth us from all sin.   *(1 John 1:7, KJV)*

It is the blood of Jesus Christ that pardons us from the acts of sin. It is also the blood of Jesus Christ that cleanses us from all indwelling sin.

> Wherefore Jesus also, that he might sanctify [cleanse] the people with his own blood, suffered without the gate.   *(Heb. 13:12, KJV)*

> What a wretched man I am! Who will rescue me from this body of death? Thanks be to God—through Jesus Christ our Lord! So then, I myself in my mind am a slave to God's law, but in the sinful nature a slave to the law of sin.   *(Rom. 7:24-25)*

For the double necessity, Jesus provided the double cure.

2. Heart Perfection. Heart perfection is the restoration of our heart to the original condition of purity of motive.

a. The heart of every Spirit-filled Christian reflects the love of God.

Heart perfection is simply a transformation of our inner nature from its hostilities, that is, hatred, pride, greed, and carnal jealousies, to a condition of divine love. John Wesley reaffirms this position.

> Both my brother [Charles Wesley] and I maintained, (1.) That Christian Perfection is that love of God and our neighbour, which implies deliverance from all sin. . . . [It is] the loving God with all our heart, mind, soul, and strength.[7]

> It is nothing higher and nothing lower than this—the pure love of God and man. . . . It is love governing the heart and life, running through all our tempers, words, and actions.[8]

The essence of heart perfection is found in the Lord's commandment of love:

> Thou shalt love the Lord thy God with all thy heart, and with all thy soul, and with all thy mind. This is the first and great commandment. And the second is like unto it, Thou shalt love thy neighbour as thyself. On these two commandments hang all the law and the prophets. *(Matt. 22:37-40, KJV)*

b. Human motives stem from our inner drives, the motivation for action, the fixation of attention and purpose. Moment-by-moment choices reveal motivation.

In the Spirit-filled life it is not our selfish will but God's will that should be the controlling motive of every confrontation. The Spirit-filled Christian must follow the example of Christ in the Garden as He prayed, "Not my will, but thine, be done" (Luke 22:42, KJV).

Having perfect motives does not guarantee perfect judgment. As long as the mind, emotions, and will are imperfectible, we will have imperfect judgment. The apostle Paul drew this distinction when he prayed:

> May God himself, the God of peace, sanctify you through and through. May your whole spirit, soul and body be kept blameless [not faultless] at the coming of our Lord Jesus Christ. *(1 Thess. 5:23)*

Thus, it needs to be clearly understood that purity of motive, not perfection of judgment, is heart perfection.

3. The Infilling of the Holy Spirit. *This gift of infilling is only possible in the absence of original sin.* That is, for our hearts to be filled with the Holy Spirit, original sin must be cleansed.

Some may argue that when we are saved, Jesus comes into our

---

7. Wesley, *Works*, 11:393-94.
8. Ibid., 397.

hearts; and when we are sanctified, the Holy Spirit comes into our hearts. But this is not biblically accurate.

Paul, in Colossians, says:

> For in Christ *all the fullness of the Deity lives* in bodily form, and *you have been given fullness in Christ,* who is the head over every power and authority.   *(2:9-10, italics added)*

Thus, when we are born again, we receive in Christ *all* of the Godhead—*Father, Son,* and *Holy Spirit.* In this state of grace, there is the coexistence of all of God and all of original sin. In this coexistent state, although we have all of God, He does not have full control of us. Until we completely surrender ourselves to God, He cannot cleanse our hearts.

Peter underscores heart cleansing as the signal event of the Day of Pentecost:

> God, who knows the heart, showed that he accepted them by giving the Holy Spirit to them, just as he did to us. He made no distinction between us and them, for *he purified their hearts by faith.*
>   *(Acts 15:8-9, italics added)*

The apostle Paul, teaching the church at Rome, makes it clear to them that the completeness of one's consecration is essential in order to experience the miracle of the full newness that is available in Christ:

> Therefore, I urge you, brothers, in view of God's mercy, to offer your bodies *as living sacrifices, holy and pleasing to God*—this is your spiritual act of worship.
>
> Do not conform any longer to the pattern of this world, but be transformed by the renewing of your mind. Then you will be able to test and approve what God's will is—his good, pleasing and perfect will.   *(Rom. 12:1-2, italics added)*

Although such diagrams are by necessity sorely simplistic, the one that follows is offered to represent the differences between the heart of the born-again Christian and that of the Spirit-filled Christian. The born-again heart illustrates the coexistence of God and the original sin in the same heart, while the Spirit-filled heart represents the absence of conflict.

Born-again Christian   Spirit-filled Christian

4. The Empowering of the Holy Spirit. The empowering that comes from the Holy Spirit is one of the most neglected areas of teaching and preaching in the evangelical world. Perhaps this is so because it is confusing to many people.

a. The Holy Spirit is a person and not just an influence.

b. Born-again believers receive the empowering of the Holy Spirit at the time they are reborn. With the coexistence of original sin and the Holy Spirit, there is conflict, and conflict causes restriction.

c. In the heart of the Spirit-filled Christian where this conflict has been cleansed, the Holy Spirit is free to empower and to influence his life in a greater measure.

d. Jesus tells us not only to be spiritually perfect but also that when we are, we will be empowered for ministry.

> Be perfect, therefore, as your heavenly Father is perfect.
> *(Matt. 5:48)*

> But *you will receive power when the Holy Spirit comes on you; and you will be my witnesses* in Jerusalem, and in all Judea and Samaria, and to the ends of the earth.   *(Acts 1:8, italics added)*

When the Holy Spirit is experienced in His fullness, that does not mean we can grow no further, nor that we have reached the zenith of spiritual growth. Rather, now that He has cleansed our hearts and is in full control of us, He can freely help us to develop our full potential.

The empowering of His Spirit is not given indiscriminately. It is given for a purpose—the distinct purpose of enabling us to live righteously and to carry out the Great Commission (see Acts 1:8).

Returning to our theological diagram, we now add the portion dealing with the Spirit-filled experience:

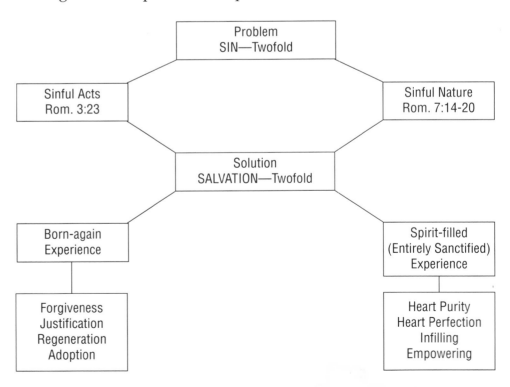

Compare the born-again and Spirit-filled life, using the following diagram.

CRISIS	CONTINUATION	CRISIS
1. Divine Initiative 2. Awareness of Need 3. Awareness of Moral Choice 4. Your Response	CONFLICT	1. Divine Initiative 2. Awareness of Need 3. Awareness of Moral Choice 4. Your Response
1. Forgiveness 2. Justification 3. Regeneration 4. Adoption	Confrontation and Temptation—Confrontation and Temptation	1. Heart Purity 2. Heart Perfection 3. Infilling of the Holy Spirit 4. Empowering of the Holy Spirit

BORN-AGAIN

SPIRIT-FILLED
(Entirely Sanctified)

Notes

To conclude this section dealing with the crisis of the Spirit-filled life, let's consider the witness of the Spirit. Just as we experienced the witness of the Holy Spirit in the born-again life, so it is experienced in the Spirit-filled life.

The Scriptures teach us that the witness of the Spirit is assured. The manner in which He gives us this witness will vary from person to person.

> Those who obey his commands live in him, and he in them. And this is how we know that he lives in us: We *know* it by the *Spirit* he *gave* us. (1 John 3:24, italics added)

> We *know* that we live in him and he in us, because he has *given* us of his *Spirit*. (1 John 4:13, italics added)

> This is the one who came by water and blood—Jesus Christ. He did not come by water only, but by water and blood. And *it is the Spirit who testifies*, because the Spirit is the truth. . . . *Anyone who believes in the Son of God has this testimony in his heart.* Anyone who does not believe God has made him out to be a liar, because he has not believed the testimony God has given about his Son. (1 John 5:6, 10, italics added)

The presence of the Spirit in our hearts is not a well-kept secret. The Spirit soon begins to manifest himself through our behavior. The fruit of the Spirit provides both internal and external evidence of the infilling of the Holy Spirit.

> But the fruit of the Spirit is love, joy, peace, patience, kindness, goodness, faithfulness, gentleness and self-control. Against such things there is no law. Those who belong to Christ Jesus have crucified the sinful nature with its passions and desires. Since we live by the Spirit, let us keep in step with the Spirit. (Gal. 5:22-25)

What joy it is when we first become aware within ourselves

that the Spirit is really producing His fruit in us. And that joy is compounded when others confirm that the Spirit is becoming observable in us! We can be tempted to let these "great beginnings" become an end in themselves. Instead, accept the challenge to let spiritual fruit bearing become your lifestyle.

II. The Continuation of the Spirit-filled Life

Just as there was spiritual growth following the crisis of the born-again life, so is there a whole world of spiritual growth awaiting us following the crisis of the Spirit-filled life. Notice the place for this growth in the diagram on the following page.

The fruit of the Spirit is an evidence of the Spirit-filled life. The fruit of the Spirit develops in one's life through growth in a variety of areas and through confrontations with temptation.

A. Growth: The way that the fruit of the Spirit is developed is through growth in the following areas.

1. A More Intense Love for His Word

As Spirit-filled Christians, we continue to mature as we develop an increased love for and application of the Word.

> Nothing is perfect except your words. Oh, how I love them. I think about them all day long. *(Ps. 119:96-97, TLB)*

2. A More Intense Love for Others

Although this imparted love is divine in its nature and quality, it can be increased in its capacity and expression.

a. We find an increased love for those in the Body of the Believers.

b. We find an increased love for those in our world who so desperately need a personal experience with Christ.

> This is the message you heard from the beginning: We should love one another. *(1 John 3:11)*

> No one has ever seen God; but if we love one another, God lives in us and his love is made complete in us. *(1 John 4:12)*

> And he has given us this command: Whoever loves God must also love his brother. *(1 John 4:21)*

3. An Eager Adjustment to New Light Revealed

We will develop an eagerness to discover new insights from God's Word. When new insights are discovered, two steps should be followed:

a. Test the insight against God's Word. Is it consistent with God's character? Is it consistent with biblical teaching?

b. If you are satisfied that the insight is indeed spiritual light, make a disciplined effort not to rationalize yourself into a position

The Christian Experience

CRISIS

1. Divine Initiative
2. Awareness of Need
3. Awareness of Moral Choice
4. Your Response

1. Forgiveness
2. Justification
3. Regeneration
4. Adoption

BORN-AGAIN

CONTINUATION

CONFLICT

Confrontation and Temptation—Confrontation and Temptation

CRISIS

1. Divine Initiative
2. Awareness of Need
3. Awareness of Moral Choice
4. Your Response

1. Heart Purity
2. Heart Perfection
3. Infilling of the Holy Spirit
4. Empowering of the Holy Spirit

SPIRIT-FILLED
(Entirely Sanctified)

CONTINUATION

ABSENCE OF CONFLICT

Confrontation and Temptation, Etc., Etc.

that is less than God's very best for you. This kind of spiritual sensitivity is not something that is always conscious; rather, it obtains from an almost intuitive sense—a deep, settled conviction that what God wants is best.

> But if we walk in the light, as he is in the light, we have fellowship with one another, and the blood of Jesus, his Son, purifies us from all sin.
> *(1 John 1:7)*

4. A More Discernible Influence and Effect of the Spirit-empowered Heart on the Amoral Functions

> *Work out* your own salvation with fear and trembling. For it is God which worketh *in* you both to will and to do of his good pleasure.
> *(Phil. 2:12-13, KJV, italics added)*

The Holy Spirit wants to change the condition of our hearts, but, more than that, He wants that change to be worked out—enfleshed—in everyday existence so that it affects every aspect of life.

a. The Spirit-filled life will have a "leveling out" or "balancing" effect on our psychical functions. The Spirit's influence will become apparent as the extreme highs and lows of our psyche tend to find a better balance.

b. The influence and effect of the Holy Spirit in some cases will even be felt in the physical area of one's life. The absence of inner moral conflict releases strength and beauty for life.

B. Confrontation and Temptation but No Conflict

Can the fruit of the Spirit develop through confrontations with temptation? How is this possible?

1. Moral growth comes through choice making. In life one is continually confronted with alternatives. These confrontations will be accompanied by varying degrees of temptation. (There is an entire chapter forthcoming, devoted to the subject of "Temptation.") There is no temptation without confrontation. In the Spirit-filled life, there will always be confrontation and temptation but without conflict. Conflict is a problem that stems from the fleshly nature.

2. The question is sometimes raised concerning the difference between the temptations of those who are Spirit-filled and those who are not. The difference lies in the fact that, in the fleshly Christian, temptation stirs up the natural corruption of the heart with its bias and bent toward sinning. However, within the heart of the Spirit-filled Christian, the tempter finds no responsive ally.

This does not mean that the Spirit-filled Christian *cannot* yield to temptation and sin; rather, the Spirit-filled Christian *need not* yield to temptation and sin. Freedom from indwelling sin serves to strengthen such a Christian in the hour of temptation. We can see now why the Spirit-filled life is an indispensable requisite to the life of constant victory over sin.

> Blessed is the man that endureth temptation: for when he is tried, he shall receive the crown of life, which the Lord hath promised to them that love him. *(James 1:12, KJV)*

3. There *will* be confrontations and temptations in the Spirit-filled life; however, since the second party in the conflict, the old fleshly nature, no longer governs the heart, there can be no conflict.

Bill Gaither, in his powerful song titled "It Is Finished," graphically portrays the conflict within the person whose heart is not totally yielded to the Lordship of the Holy Spirit. But as the song continues to unfold, he does not leave the conflict unresolved; he announces that victory is possible for the asking: Jesus can be not only Savior but also Lord.

> *Yet in my heart a battle was raging,*
>   *Not all pris'ners of war had come home.*
> *They were battlefields of my own making,*
>   *I didn't know that the war had been won.*
>
> *Then I heard that the King of the ages*
>   *Had fought all the battles for me.*
> *And vict'ry was mine for the asking,*
>   *And now, praise His name, I am free!*
>
> *It is finished, the battle is over.*
>   *It is finished, there'll be no more war.*
> *It is finished, the end of the conflict.*
>   *It is finished, and Jesus is Lord.*
> *He is Lord!*
>   *He is Lord!*
>   *He is Lord!**

III. The Concerns Regarding the Spirit-filled Life

The following are some representative questions from Christians regarding the Spirit-filled life.

A. "What are the differences between the amoral and moral natures of human beings?"

The crisis of the Spirit-filled life changes the *moral condition* of the heart. The body and the soul are only affected indirectly by a changed heart. For example, a less conflict-ridden heart will tend to reduce physiological stress.

---

*Copyright 1976 by William J. Gaither. International Copyright Secured. All Rights Reserved. Used by Special Permission of the Publisher.

Our heart represents our moral nature; for the decisions and actions of the heart we are accountable to God. One's amoral nature concerns matters other than issues of right and wrong—matters such as learning how cognitive processes work, selecting the color of paint for one's closet, and deciding to mow the lawn before fertilizing it. (See chapter 3 for a review of human nature.)

B. "How can one know that he or she is Spirit-filled?"

In chapter 4 we learned that sin is twofold, comprised of the acts of sin and the nature of sin. The acts of sin are those choices that we have made against the will of God. The fleshly nature is the original tendency toward sinning with which we were born. When we are born again, we confess our sins (the acts) and accept by faith Christ's forgiveness of our sins.

> If we confess our sins, he is faithful and just and will forgive us our sins and purify us from all unrighteousness.   *(1 John 1:9)*

The Spirit-filled crisis follows essentially the same steps as the born-again life. We consecrate our hearts to God, and He cleanses or purifies them. Just as we accept Christ's forgiveness by faith, so we accept His cleansing of the heart by faith.

> God, who knows the heart, showed that he accepted them by giving the Holy Spirit to them, just as he did to us. He made no distinction between us and them, for he purified their hearts by faith.
> *(Acts 15:8-9)*

C. "When can one be filled with the Spirit?"

There are occasions when people have been filled with the Spirit soon after conversion; with others, the interval has been longer.

In Acts 9:1-16 we read how the apostle Paul came to believe in Jesus. In the very next verse (17), Paul was filled with the Holy Spirit. This occurred only a short time after his conversion.

There is no required time interval for this experience. The important thing is to know that we *can* be filled with the Holy Spirit. Once we perceive the need, the experience is for us.

D. "What are the major theories for dealing with original sin taught by most Evangelicals?"

In what might be called the evangelical world there are essentially three theological positions held concerning original sin with respect to the Spirit-filled life.

All Christians believe that:

1. After the born-again crisis there remains in the heart of the believer the presence of original sin.

2. Original sin must be cleansed before anyone can enter heaven. No sin can enter heaven.

The real difference in the three theological positions concerns: When is original sin dealt with—in this life or at death?

By employing the threefold function view diagram, perhaps we can make each theological position understandable.

1. There are those who believe that we are born again and filled with the Holy Spirit at the moment of conversion.

a. Those who subscribe to this theory believe that original sin is "inseparably and unalterably" a part of the human nature—body and soul, as well as spirit. They believe that the body is not only affected but also infected.

b. They believe that the fleshly nature dies at the moment the body dies and not before.

Diagrammatically, even after we are Spirit-filled, we look like this:

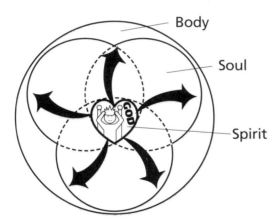

Note: The dark arrows represent the sinful affects and infection of a life with self at the center.

2. There are those who believe that after we are born again, there is a further work of God in the heart, the infilling of the Holy Spirit. Even though these people believe this to be a second crisis experience, they do not believe that original sin is cleansed. They believe that the infilling only provides more power to live a more victorious life.

This group of Christians is generally divided into two schools of thought:

a. Those who believe that original sin is inseparably a part of one's total being—physical, psychical, and spiritual.

Diagrammatically, it would look like this:

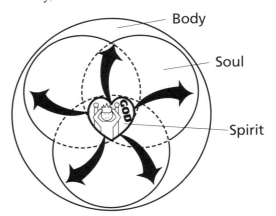

b. Those who believe that original sin resides only in the spirit and does not infect the body or the soul. The diagram for this group looks like this:

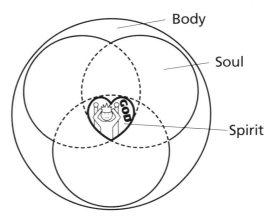

There are several things to keep in mind in understanding these differences.

(1) Those in the first group believe:

    (a) that the Spirit-filled experience is subsequent to the born-again experience

    (b) that original sin resides in the body and soul and therefore cannot be cleansed in this life

(2) Those in the second group believe:

    (a) that the Spirit-filled experience is subsequent to the born-again experience

    (b) that original sin resides, not in the body or soul, but only in the spirit. The Spirit-filled experience gives one more power and various gifts, but original sin is never fully cleansed from the heart.

3. There are those who believe that after the born-again life there is the further work of God in one's heart, the infilling of the Holy Spirit. They believe that original sin resides only in the human heart and is cleansed by the work of the Holy Spirit.

a. There are several considerations held by this position that need to be clarified:

    (1) This position does not suggest that we cannot be tempted (Heb. 4:14-15);

    (2) nor, that because we are filled with the Spirit, we can no longer sin;

    (3) nor, does it suggest that, by being filled with the Spirit, we will be perfect in either our physical or psychical nature.

b. This theological position does believe that when the heart is cleansed by the infilling of the Holy Spirit:

    (1) there is no longer any conflict between original sin and Christ;

    (2) with this conflict gone, we can turn our energies to a more rapid spiritual growth;

    (3) we are able to discover a new intimacy in our relationship with God;

    (4) the degree of imbalance in our psychical functions will be greatly diminished by the influence of the Spirit's uncontested control of one's heart;

    (5) there is not that inner ally (original sin) of the heart with which Satan can establish a foothold to defeat us.

Diagrammatically, this theological position looks like this:

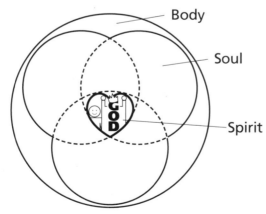

The heart is pure, though the body and soul are imperfect.

As a sincere Christian, always desire God's best. Study the differences between these positions, and thereby avoid confusion and trouble.

E. "Does God have a different standard of living for the fleshly Christian?"

There are many born-again Christians who have the misconception that because they are not filled with the Holy Spirit, the level of their Christian lives, so far as obedience to God is concerned, is different and not so demanding as is the life of the Spirit-filled Christian.

This is a unbiblical position; it carries with it implications that could prove harmful to the Christian personally as well as those we influence.

The scripture is clear:

> No one who is born of God will continue to sin.   *(1 John 3:9)*

Disobedience is sin, and sin separates us from God (see Isa. 59:2).

F. "Is it possible that restitution may be a requirement of the Spirit-filled life?"

Yes, it may. Every Christian, whether fleshly or Spirit-filled, is a representative to the world of who Christ is. As His representative we should be concerned about living up to the claims of the Lordship of Christ in our lives.

But if one is a fleshly Christian, several problems are posed:

1. The heart is diseased, selfish, and contrary to Christ's best. One's attitudes toward God's will and the people around us may reflect poorly on Christ.

2. Simply to recognize these bad attitudes and conditions and say, "God, please cleanse me of all this pollution," is not always adequate.

  a. What about the sorrow we've caused God?

  b. What about the hurt we've created for others?

The willingness to make restitution, both to God and our fellow human beings as light is revealed, is a must if we are to enjoy a life filled with God's Spirit.

> Therefore, if you are offering your gift at the altar and there remember that your brother has something against you, leave your gift there in front of the altar. First go and be reconciled to your brother; then come and offer your gift.   *(Matt. 5:23-24)*

G. "Can we sin after we are filled with the Spirit?"

Many Evangelicals hold the erroneous view that Spirit-filled Christians believe themselves to be immune to sin. Being Spirit-filled does not short-circuit one's power to choose. We still have the capacity to choose to sin. The difference the Spirit-filled life provides is that, with the absence of inner conflict, there comes added power to live the victorious, Spirit-filled life.

H. "How do we resolve the apparent contradiction between total surrender and personal ambition in the Spirit-filled life?"

Those totally surrendered to God are so excited about doing His will that, once they know His will, they are eager to pursue it; there is neither lack of ambition nor settling for mediocrity.

Personal ambition is never at a higher pitch than when one's will is surrendered to God.

I. "How does one lose and/or regain the Spirit-filled life?"

1. In the beginning Adam and Eve possessed moral perfection. How did they lose this condition? By sinning against the known will of God. Likewise, the way by which we lose this moral perfection is by sinning against the known will of God.

> Remember, too, that knowing what is right to do and then not doing it is sin. *(James 4:17, TLB)*

2. We regain the Spirit-filled life, first, by repenting of sins and, when necessary, making restitution. Second, we must consecrate our hearts to God.

Both of these experiences are completed by faith in what Christ did for us on the Cross.

> For it is by grace you have been saved, through faith—and this not from yourselves, it is the gift of God. *(Eph. 2:8)*

> And so Jesus also suffered outside the city gate to make the people holy through his own blood. *(Heb. 13:12)*

J. "Can the Holy Spirit leave us?"

In Rom. 8:38-39, Paul shows us that no external force can separate us from the love of God. But the Holy Spirit can leave us if we turn our backs on Him. However, He will not leave us if we are obedient to Him.

K. "How much does one's personality change when one is Spirit-filled?"

The personality of the individual involves the abilities, interests, and attributes that makes one person different from another. This includes the total physical, intellectual, emotional, volitional, and spiritual capacities of the individual. In the Spirit-filled life the essential change that occurs is that the seat of the affections or heart of a person is purified, and decisions and directions one chooses will be no longer self-centered but Christ-centered.

This basic change will only affect these abilities, interests, and attributes in the way they relate to God's will.

L. "What does 'total commitment' mean?"

Total commitment means that body, soul, and spirit are completely given to God's ownership. The will of one's life has been voluntarily and completely surrendered in favor of God's will.

In a later chapter on "Commitment," we will deal further with this subject.

M. "Can a Spirit-filled person experience depression?"

Current research indicates that some forms of depression emanate from physiological chemical imbalances; others are the result of genetic predispositions. In other words, not all forms of depression arise from spiritual impoverishment; the body and even the soul are the sources of forms of depression that are amoral in nature. For example, colors in a room may affect one's disposition. Weather changes may cause people to have feelings of depression. Depression may be a result of chemical changes or cycles that occur in human bodies. There are many other factors that may effect physical, mental, and emotional depression.

There is no reason to feel guilt about amoral forms of depression. However, this type of depression must be distinguished from spiritual depression, which *can* be a result of a sinful response in one's life.

Spiritual depression is often a result of an act of disobedience or failing to respond in a timely manner to what God has revealed. This moral, spiritual depression comes as a result of guilt in one's life.

It is important to know that depression experienced in the body or soul functions, if not dealt with, can have a detrimental effect on one's spiritual life. The more control the Holy Spirit has of one's heart, the more readily the soul function of the individual can be improved and depression lessened.

N. "What is the problem when one has a bad spirit?"

Generally speaking, a bad spirit is a spiritual condition in which the Holy Spirit is not in complete control. In this condition, self reigns supreme and is usually evidenced by attitudes of self-defense, negative responses, or other carnal behavior.

O. "Is it possible to be born again and Spirit-filled simultaneously?"

Simultaneous means "two or more events happening at the same instant." We stated earlier that when we have Christ, we have all the Godhead—Father, Son, and Holy Spirit (Col. 2:9-10). We reaffirm our faith in this position. When we become born again, we have all of God, but the mixedness of our hearts prevents us from giving all of the self to Him. It takes some time after being born again before we discover the conflict within us. Once we awaken to our need and discover God's provision for us, we are candidates for the Spirit-filled life.

P. "What is the difference between initial sanctification and entire sanctification?"

Both initial and entire sanctification are acts of the Holy Spirit. We will find both of these terms used repeatedly in the writings of John Wesley.

Quite simply, initial sanctification refers to the born-again experience in which the Holy Spirit comes into one's heart in forgiveness, justification, regeneration, and adoption. The fleshly nature, however, remains. Entire sanctification refers to the work of the Holy Spirit in the Spirit-filled experience in which He cleanses away fleshly pollution, perfecting the moral motivation, entirely controlling the heart, and empowering believers for service.

> Initial or partial sanctification includes in its scope all that acquired pollution which attaches to the sinner's own acts; while entire sanctification includes the cleansing from original sin or inherited depravity.[9]

Q. "Is it true that only Jesus comes into one's heart in the born-again experience, then the Holy Spirit comes in at the time of sanctification?"

The answer is no. If we receive God the Son into our hearts at the time of the born-again experience and God the Holy Spirit at the time of sanctification, then when do we receive God the Father? As Paul states:

> For in Christ all the fullness of the Deity lives in bodily form, and you have been given fullness in Christ, who is the head over every power and authority.   *(Col. 2:9-10)*

Here is another way of expressing that same thought:

> For in Christ there is all of God in a human body; *so you have everything when you have Christ,* and you are filled with God through your union with Christ.   *(TLB)*

When Christ comes into one's heart, all of the Godhead is there, not just part of Him. Both the born-again experience, as well

---

9. Wiley, *Christian Theology,* 2:481.

as the Spirit-filled experience, are works of the Holy Spirit. Sanctification begins in conversion. The problems of the converted life stems from the fact that, after the born-again experience, all of the selfish, fleshly nature also remains in the heart. As was once stated, "The Holy Spirit is 'Resident' but not 'President.'"

All orthodox Christianity believes that after the born-again experience there still remains the presence of original sin. The real question centers around the idea of *when* we can be freed from this internal civil war caused by the coexistence of both flesh and Spirit. The good news is that we do not have to wait until physical death frees us, but rather, we can know the cleansing, empowering fullness of the Holy Spirit in this present life.

Without the presence of the Holy Spirit, we would never have the power to appropriate the Lordship of the Holy Spirit for the Spirit-filled experience.

> No one can say, "Jesus is Lord," except by the Holy Spirit.
>
> *(1 Cor. 12:3)*

In the born-again life we have all of the Godhead in us. But when we recognize the warring within, He reveals to us the possibilities of peace; as we acknowledge, confess, commit, and believe, we receive Him in His fullness. *He* finally has all of *us.*

Review Exercise

Divide your group into pairs, and have each couple draw the diagram of THE CHRISTIAN EXPERIENCE. Be sure to include

1. Crisis of the Born-again Life

    a. Four areas of response

    b. Four areas of result

2. Continuation

    a. Confrontation

    b. Temptation

3. Conflict

4. Crisis of the Spirit-filled (Sanctified) Life

    a. Four areas of response

    b. Four areas of result

5. Continuation

    a. Confrontation

    b. Temptation

Now, turn to the person next to you, and explain the process of the Christian experience.

Summary

How does one reconcile the presence of sin in the lives of Christians? The early leaders of the church took a variety of stances to deal with this problem. The philosophical view of Augustine took the position that the flesh itself was sinful; therefore, one would never be free from sin in this present life. Others within the ranks of the church felt that holiness was possible, but only by being neither of the world nor in the world; they chose to lead a monastic life, cloistered away from the problems of the real world. By leading a life of prayer, Bible reading, and meditation, shutting out all vain and worldly thoughts, they strove to achieve spiritual perfection.

An earlier view offered by the Shepherd of Hermas in the second century was that a life of sinlessness should be the norm. Yet, if a believer sinned, forgiveness would be possible. This view, which continued up into the sixth century, suffered misinterpretations. But its purest form could be found in the doctrine of John Wesley.

Wesley taught the doctrine that a second definite work of grace, following regeneration, was possible in which we believers are free to not sin; we are free from the bondage to the deadly lower nature. This work of grace has been made available by divine initiative. In His death on the Cross, not only did Jesus pay our debt for sins committed, but also He defeated the powers of sin, death, and hell. His sacrifice broke the power of sin in the flesh, freeing us from ever having to sin again. His sacrifice destroyed the fleshly nature, the sin principle, that "responsive ally" within us, setting us free from enslavement to sin. God took that kind of initiative in our behalf. But for the miracle to take place within us requires our response of faith.

When this work has been accomplished in our hearts, the results are heart purity (our hearts are cleansed of fleshly corruption by the blood of the Lamb), heart perfection (the Spirit restores our motive life so that what we desire comes from purity of intent), infilling of the Holy Spirit (our hearts having been cleansed of corruption, He now has all of us as we have all of Him), and empowering of the Holy Spirit (without the presence of inner conflict within us, the Spirit empowers us for works of ministry).

As we continue on, we discover some marvelous benefits of the Spirit-filled life: the fruit of the Spirit is evidenced in our life; we develop an intense love for His Word; our love for others deepens; we pursue more light from Him so that we may draw closer to Him; and even the amoral psychical functions of our life become more balanced.

Another immediately discernible benefit is that, although we continue to face temptation, we face it with the absence of conflict.

Notes

The first five chapters have dealt with the foundational elements of becoming a Spirit-filled disciple. The remaining chapters are given largely to helping disciples achieve God's plan for their lives. Before proceeding, it is important that we have gained all that God has for us in the first five chapters. Let's review these four points.

1. The premise for discipling is " _____
_____ _____ _____."

2. The source to which we turn for discovering how to become a disciple is _____ _____ _____
_____.

3. The problem we face in becoming all God wants us to be is our _____ _____.
In our present study we are presenting the idea that human beings may best be understood as _____ _____.

4. The solution for our problem is twofold: God's provision through the _____-_____ _____
and the _____-_____ _____.

6

Faith

Introduction

Summary

Faith is the gift of God resulting in the capacity to believe that which we cannot see and to act upon that belief.

6

Faith

Perhaps the best-known description of faith is the King James Version of Heb. 11:1:

> Now faith is the substance of things hoped for, the evidence of things not seen.

Few subjects are more misunderstood than faith. The purpose of this present chapter is to make faith clear and usable.

In God's Word, some startling statements are made about faith:

> And *without faith it is impossible to please God,* because anyone who comes to him must believe that he exists and that he rewards those who earnestly seek him. *(Heb. 11:6, italics added)*

> In the same way, *faith* by itself, if it is *not accompanied by action, is dead.* *(James 2:17, italics added)*

> But the man who has doubts is condemned if he eats, because his eating is not from faith; and *everything that does not come from faith is sin.* *(Rom. 14:23, italics added)*

If "without faith it is impossible to please God," then we must make some radical discoveries about faith if we are to tap the potential God has for us and live a life acceptable to Him. In the remainder of this chapter we will investigate what faith is and how we can please God by using it properly.

I. Faith Explained

A. The Definition of Faith

Faith is the gift of God resulting in the capacity to believe that which we cannot see and to act upon that belief. Faith is a uniquely human function; the diagram below helps to illustrate this point.

1. Faith involves the mind, emotions, and will, working in concert together.

   a. "The capacity to believe" is possible because you have a *mind*—the capacity to understand and reason.

   b. "The capacity to believe" is possible, also, because you have *emotions*—the capacity to feel deeply.

   c. "The capacity to believe that which we cannot see and to act upon that belief" is possible because you have *will*—the capacity to act.

2. Other factors in this definition of faith are:

   a. Faith involves all the functions of the soul.

   b. Faith is used in both the moral and amoral aspects of life.

Illustration:

When you speak of having faith in a pilot and airplane to get you from Denver to Los Angeles, you are not using the spirit function of the mind, emotions, and will. You are using, rather, the human function of the brain, which has the capacity to think, feel, and act in the amoral areas of life.

In contrast to this:

When you acknowledge that on the Cross Jesus Christ took upon himself your sins and you respond by trusting Him to forgive you of your sins, this act of faith is made possible by God's grace. It appropriates in your heart forgiveness, justification, regeneration, and adoption. In this case you are using the spirit function of the mind, emotions, and will.

What is the determining factor that distinguishes issues of the heart from issues of the soul? Heb. 4:12 ascribes unto the Word of God the ability to make such delineations:

> The word of God is living and active. Sharper than any double-edged sword, it penetrates even to dividing soul and spirit, joints and marrow; it judges the thoughts and attitudes of the heart.

God's Word is the determining factor as to which of these functions is in operation.

(1) A moral choice is not involved in choosing one airline over another.

(2) Choosing the Lord Jesus Christ over Buddhism or Islam is a moral choice.

Again, faith is a gift of grace providing "the capacity to believe that which we cannot see and to act upon that belief."

When the object of one's belief is the Word of God, scriptures such as Rom. 10:17, "Faith cometh by hearing, and hearing by the word of God" begin to make a very practical difference in your life.

B. The Confusion Surrounding Faith

When one does not clearly understand the meaning of faith, confusion results. Some of the most prevalent marks of this confusion are seen in the following:

1. The idea that you don't have enough faith

2. The idea that some people have more faith than others

3. The idea that faith is a fragile commodity

4. The idea that faith is a deep emotional tingle

5. The idea that faith comes as a result of long hours of penance

Stop and analyze this definition of *faith* for a moment: "Faith is . . . the capacity to believe that which we cannot see and to act upon that belief."

a. Your problem is not that you don't have enough faith; you have all the faith you need. The real issue is whether or not this faith is operating properly.

b. If you are truly motivated to act upon your beliefs, you must be certain that your beliefs are founded upon the Word of God.

Let's compare our definition of faith to some verses on faith:

● "Now faith is the substance of things hoped for, the evidence of things not seen" (Heb. 11:1, KJV).

"The substance of things hoped for, the evidence of things not seen"—these two phrases convey the same thought: Faith is the capacity to believe that which we cannot see and to step out upon that belief.

● "Faith cometh by hearing, and hearing by the word of God" (Rom. 10:17, KJV).

When you desire to be rid of the sin you have been carrying, and through the Word of God you learn that Jesus' shed blood is the provision that's already been made, then you ask for His forgiveness. This is what it means to be born again; the process: hearing, believing, and acting.

● It is no mystery why faith is more operative in some people than others. You see, faith is "the capacity to believe that which we cannot see and to act upon that belief." If the capacities of mind, emotions, and will are cluttered with all kinds of pressures and problems, it makes sense that they will not generate the robust faith necessary to live God's way.

When you are able to identify clutter and its effects in your life, you are not so tempted to blame God for the pressures you are feeling; you are not so tempted to give up and quit. Rather, you realize that you need to make some changes in your life if you are going to be victorious.

To increase faith's operational potential:

a. Pray specifically about spiritual clutter in your life.

b. Get into the Word of God with a new intensity.

c. Analyze your financial income and outgo.

d. Seek godly counsel if necessary.

e. You are developing plans to deliver yourself from ineffective faith.

f. Faith is not your problem; your problem is rather the restrictions to your faith.

Evaluating the clutter in our lives is a worthwhile enterprise. Take a moment for the exercise below.

> Jot down two things you are going to do to clear out the clutter in your life—clutter that weakens your faith:
>
> 1.
>
> 2.

II. Faith Is a Gift of Grace

Faith provides "the capacity to believe that which we cannot see and to act upon that belief." It is not something:

- That is determined at birth.
- That varies with personality type.
- That is affected by the stars.
- That is tied to your physical health.

Faith is God's gift to us. The capacity to receive faith was given at creation.

Gen. 1:26 says, "Let us make man in our image." If we were created in God's own image, then we are intelligent, emotional, and volitional. That is, we have a mind, emotions, and will. With these come "the capacity to believe that which we cannot see and to act upon that belief."

Here are two illustrations that differentiate between the gift of faith and human trust.

- Suppose you believe it is wise to invest $1,000 in General Motors stock. You have not only the capacity to believe but also the capacity to act upon that belief. That is called faith: faith in General Motors stock. To choose between investing in General Motors or the Ford Company is not, however, a moral issue.

Faith, or in this case, human trust, *is the bridge of action* that causes you to move from this mere consideration to the actual writing of that check and investing in General Motors.

- Likewise, when an unbeliever hears the good news of salvation, it is faith given by God's grace that enables active belief in Jesus.

This capacity is not something you learn or earn—it is the gift of God's grace.

Number 1

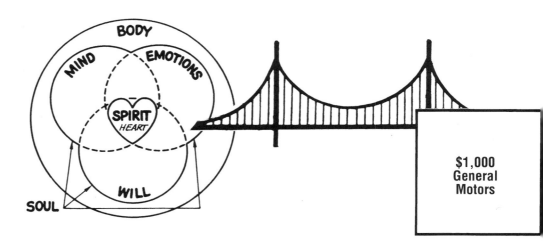

This diagram illustrates the amoral decision or action of investing $1,000 in General Motors instead of the Ford Company, a decision that has nothing to do with morality—only human judgment.

Number 2

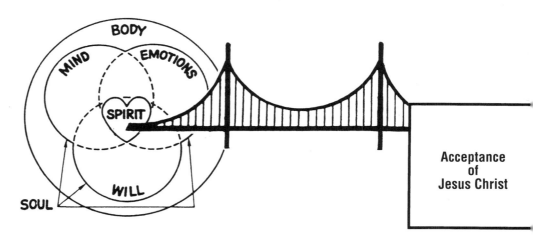

This diagram illustrates the unbeliever's decision (after hearing or reading the story of salvation through Christ) to act upon that truth by trusting in Jesus.

Remember: the capacity to believe that which we cannot see and to act upon that belief is a gift of God's grace.

III. Faith as the Way to Life

There are two aspects to the life of faith. One has to do with entering into this new life, and the other concerns how to live by faith in this new life. Let's concern ourselves first with entering into this life of faith in Jesus.

A. Life in Jesus Christ

There is no way of entering into this life except through faith in Jesus. There are many scriptures that indicate this truth:

> For God so loved the world that he gave his one and only Son, that whoever believes in him shall not perish but have eternal life.
> *(John 3:16)*

> For God did not send his Son into the world to condemn the world, but to save the world through him.   *(John 3:17)*

> This righteousness from God comes through faith in Jesus Christ to all who believe.   *(Rom. 3:22)*

> For it is by grace you have been saved, through faith—and this not from yourselves, it is the gift of God.   *(Eph. 2:8)*

> For it is with your heart that you believe and are justified, and it is with your mouth that you confess and are saved. As the Scripture says, "Anyone who trusts in him will never be put to shame."
> *(Rom. 10:10-11)*

The Word of God is likewise clear in its proclamation that just as we are saved by faith, so are we filled with the Holy Spirit by faith. Much of the confusion surrounding the Spirit-filled life stems back to a lack of understanding that we enter into this fullness of the Spirit by faith and not by growth.

Peter testifies that the critical issue concerning Gentile believers is not that they meet Jewish standards but rather that they have received the Holy Spirit. How? "By faith!"

> God, who knows the heart, showed that he accepted them by giving the Holy Spirit to them, just as he did to us. He made no distinction between us and them, for he purified their hearts *by faith*."
> *(Acts 15:8-9, italics added)*

Paul, in referring back to his own experience of being filled with the Holy Spirit and receiving the call of God to preach pardon and purity, made this statement in Acts 26:17-18:

> I am sending you to them to open their eyes and turn them from darkness to light, and from the power of Satan to God, so that they may receive forgiveness of sins and a place among those who are sanctified *by faith in me*.   *(italics added)*

This, the key to entering into life with God, is clearly and unquestionably the act of faith—"the capacity to believe that which we cannot see and to act upon that belief."

Have you ever worked with those who seemed to have a difficult time entering into this life with God? Have you had this problem yourself?

Is it because you lack "the capacity to believe that which [you] cannot see and to act upon that belief"? Certainly not. Let's look at some issues that sometimes obstruct the life of faith. These may include:

- Preconceived notions that you are unable to make necessary restitution

- The embarrassment of making restitution

- The lack of understanding the gospel

- The misconception of faith

- Preconceived notions as to what being a Christian is

- Preconceived notions as to what being a Christian would cost

- The "weird ways" of other Christians (so-called?)

- The presence of selfishness and pride in your heart

- The desire to have God's will—your way

Write in the box below three reasons you have observed that people have a difficult time entering into this new life of faith:

> 1.
>
> 2.
>
> 3.

B. Living the Life of Faith

Now that you have entered into this life in Christ, you should consider what it means to live out this life of faith.

The apostle Paul spoke to the beginning believers of the Colossian church about this very matter of continuing to live this life of faith.

> So then, just as you received Christ Jesus as Lord, continue to live in him, rooted and built up in him, strengthened in the faith as you were taught, and overflowing with thankfulness.
>
> See to it that no one takes you captive through hollow and deceptive philosophy, which depends on human tradition and the basic principles of this world rather than on Christ.
>
> For in Christ all the fullness of the Deity lives in bodily form, and you have been given fullness in Christ, who is the head over every power and authority.
>
> In him you were also circumcised, in the putting off of the sinful nature, not with a circumcision done by the hands of men but with the circumcision done by Christ, having been buried with him in baptism and raised with him through your faith in the power of God, who raised him from the dead.

When you were dead in your sins and in the uncircumcision of your sinful nature, God made you alive with Christ. He forgave us all our sins, having canceled the written code, with its regulations, that was against us and that stood opposed to us; he took it away, nailing it to the cross. And having disarmed the powers and authorities, he made a public spectacle of them, triumphing over them by the cross.

Therefore do not let anyone judge you by what you eat or drink, or with regard to a religious festival, a New Moon celebration or a Sabbath day. These are a shadow of the things that were to come; the reality, however, is found in Christ. Do not let anyone who delights in false humility and the worship of angels disqualify you for the prize. Such a person goes into great detail about what he has seen, and his unspiritual mind puffs him up with idle notions. He has lost connection with the Head, from whom the whole body, supported and held together by its ligaments and sinews, grows as God causes it to grow.

Since you died with Christ to the basic principles of this world, why, as though you still belonged to it, do you submit to its rules: "Do not handle! Do not taste! Do not touch!"? These are all destined to perish with use, because they are based on human commands and teachings. Such regulations indeed have an appearance of wisdom, with their self-imposed worship, their false humility and their harsh treatment of the body, but they lack any value in restraining sensual indulgence.   *(Col. 2:6-23)*

Since, then, you have been raised with Christ, set your hearts on things above, where Christ is seated at the right hand of God. Set your minds on things above, not on earthly things. For you died, and your life is now hidden with Christ in God. When Christ, who is your life, appears, then you also will appear with him in glory.   *(Col. 3:1-4)*

Do not give way to the tendency to complicate the life of faith. Difficulty in one's faith-life is not resolved by praying, "Lord, give me more faith," but rather, asking God to help you identify the reasons why your faith is not operating properly. These reasons (clutter, pressures, the need for more of God's Word) not only are understandable but also can be resolved quickly.

Making faith too complicated often results in misdirected faith.

Here are some examples of misdirected faith:

● If you believe some have been given more faith than others, you may be tempted to think you don't have enough. As a result, you will live below what God has for you.

● You may believe that you can just pray, and God will give you more faith. When a prayer is not answered, you may suspect that God treats others better than you.

● If you believe that faith is a deep emotional catharsis, you may find yourself straining to achieve a certain emotional state. Your goal becomes misdirected.

Just as blood carries oxygen to all the parts of your body, so faith carries God's best to your life. If the veins of your life are cluttered by all kinds of pressures, problems, and procrastinations, then don't expect to live at the level of Christian happiness and fulfill-ment God has for you. Strive instead to simplify your life, so that faith may flow unobstructed, and the image of God's Spirit may be seen in you.

IV. Faith on Three Levels

Faith can operate at differing levels of effectiveness. The Bible tells us that faith functions on three levels of effectiveness:

Little Faith

Great Faith

Perfect Faith

A. Little Faith

Little Faith can also be called selfish faith; it is faith that exclusively considers one's own need.

Some people have the idea that *selfish* and *sinful* are the same, but this is not necessarily true. *Selfish* means "exclusively consider-ing one's own need." This is an important distinction to be made; otherwise, you will suffer some pains of false guilt that will be harmful to your growth.

There are three places in the New Testament where it speaks of Little Faith. Two are listed below:

1. Matthew 8:23-26

> Then he got into the boat and his disciples followed him. Without warning, a furious storm came up on the lake, so that the waves swept over the boat. But Jesus was sleeping. The disciples went and woke him, saying, "Lord, save us! We're going to drown!"
>
> He replied, "You of little faith, why are you so afraid?" Then he got up and rebuked the winds and the waves, and it was completely calm.

Notice two things:

a. The request they made was exclusively for themselves.

b. Their cry for help was a call of faith, and they did receive.

2. Matthew 14:22-33, KJV

> And straightway Jesus constrained his disciples to get into a ship, and to go before him unto the other side, while he sent the multitudes away.
>
> And when he had sent the multitudes away, he went up into a mountain apart to pray: and when the evening was come, he was there alone.

But the ship was now in the midst of the sea, tossed with waves; for the wind was contrary.

And in the fourth watch of the night Jesus went unto them, walking on the sea.

And when the disciples saw him walking on the sea, they were troubled, saying, It is a spirit; and they cried out for fear.

But straightway Jesus spake unto them, saying, Be of good cheer; it is I; be not afraid.

And Peter answered him and said, Lord, if it be thou, bid me come unto thee on the water.

And he said, Come. And when Peter was come down out of the ship, he walked on the water, to go to Jesus.

But when he saw the wind boisterous, he was afraid; and beginning to sink, he cried, saying, Lord, save me.

And immediately Jesus stretched forth his hand, and caught him, and said unto him, O thou of little faith, wherefore didst thou doubt?

And when they were come into the ship, the wind ceased.

Then they that were in the ship came and worshipped him, saying, Of a truth thou art the Son of God.

The same two observations can be made of this passage:

a. Their request was made exclusively on their own behalf.

b. Nevertheless it was a cry of faith, and they did receive.

As good as Little Faith is, let's look at a level of faith that is far better.

B. Great Faith

The characteristic of Little Faith is that it is concerned with selfish interests. Great Faith is selfless faith, and it is available to all.

Notice on whose behalf faith is being exercised in these examples:

1. Matthew 8:5-13, KJV

And when Jesus was entered into Capernaum, there came unto him a centurion, beseeching him,

And saying, Lord, my servant lieth at home sick of the palsy, grievously tormented.

And Jesus saith unto him, I will come and heal him.

The centurion answered and said, Lord, I am not worthy that thou shouldest come under my roof: but speak the word only, and my servant shall be healed.

For I am a man under authority, having soldiers under me; and I say to this man, Go, and he goeth; and to another, Come, and he cometh; and to my servant, Do this, and he doeth it.

When Jesus heard it, he marvelled, and said to them that followed, Verily I say unto you, I have not found so great faith, no, not in Israel.

And I say unto you, That many shall come from the east and west, and shall sit down with Abraham, and Isaac, and Jacob, in the kingdom of heaven.

But the children of the kingdom shall be cast out into outer darkness: there shall be weeping and gnashing of teeth.

And Jesus said unto the centurion, Go thy way; and as thou hast believed, so be it done unto thee. And his servant was healed in the selfsame hour.

Notice the difference:

a. Faith was being exercised in the interest of someone else.

b. It was a faith that produced an observable response.

2. Matthew 15:21-28, KJV

Then Jesus went thence, and departed into the coasts of Tyre and Sidon.

And, behold, a woman of Canaan came out of the same coasts, and cried unto him, saying, Have mercy on me, O Lord, thou son of David; my daughter is grievously vexed with a devil.

But he answered her not a word. And his disciples came and besought him, saying, Send her away; for she crieth after us.

But he answered and said, I am not sent but unto the lost sheep of the house of Israel.

Then came she and worshipped him, saying, Lord, help me.

But he answered and said, It is not meet to take the children's bread, and to cast it to dogs.

And she said, Truth, Lord: yet the dogs eat of the crumbs which fall from their masters' table.

Then Jesus answered and said unto her, O woman, great is thy faith: be it unto thee even as thou wilt. And her daughter was made whole from that very hour.

In this story, too,

a. The prayer was offered in the interest of someone else.

b. The faith in that prayer took hold, and the results were evident.

C. Perfect Faith

The issue of whether we are saved by faith or by our good works has been the subject of controversy down through the years. Most Evangelicals today understand that, though we are saved by grace through faith, yet as faith is operative in our lives, it produces many works.

James, the brother of Jesus, offers some instruction about the relationship between faith and works:

What doth it profit, my brethren, though a man say he hath faith, and have not works? can faith save him?

If a brother or sister be naked, and destitute of daily food,

And one of you say unto them, Depart in peace, be ye warmed and filled; notwithstanding ye give them not those things which are needful to the body; what doth it profit?

Even so faith, if it hath not works, is dead, being alone.

> Yea, a man may say, Thou hast faith, and I have works: shew me thy faith without thy works, and I will shew thee my faith by my works.
>
> Thou believest that there is one God; thou doest well: the devils also believe, and tremble.
>
> But wilt thou know, O vain man, that faith without works is dead? *(James 2:14-20, KJV)*

You have seen Little Faith—this is selfish faith, faith for one's own interest. You have seen Great Faith—this is selfless faith, exercised in the interest of others.

Now consider Perfect Faith or Complete Faith, which can be described as sacrificial faith.

James continues his lesson:

> Was not Abraham our father justified by works, when he had offered Isaac his son upon the altar?
>
> Seest thou how faith wrought with his works, and by works was faith made perfect?
>
> And the scripture was fulfilled which saith, Abraham believed God, and it was imputed unto him for righteousness: and he was called the Friend of God. *(vv. 21-23, KJV)*

Gen. 22 records what Abraham did that was so remarkable that it should be ascribed to him that his faith was perfect, or complete.

There are at least five steps in the method of Abraham's Perfect Faith:

The Five Steps in Abraham's Faith
1.
2.
3.
4.
5.

Now list at least three signs of God's response:

The Three Signs of God's Response
1.
2.
3.

So the issue is not whether you have faith at all, nor is it the kind of faith you have.

Rather, because Christians may function on three levels of

faith, the challenge is to develop a life where most of your experiences are of the Perfect Faith and Great Faith quality.

There is nothing sinful about Little Faith. However, to aspire to Great Faith and Perfect Faith should be the goal of every Christian.

Summary

Just as you were born again by faith, so you become Spirit-filled by faith. Furthermore, your daily walk with the Lord is a result of faith. The whole plan of redemption is accomplished from start to finish by faith.

What is faith? It is "the substance of things hoped for, the evidence of things not seen" (Heb. 11:1, KJV). It is "the capacity to believe that which we cannot see and to act upon that belief."

Faith, while similar to human trust, is operationally similar but qualitatively different. By grace God gives us faith—all the faith we'll ever need. Effective faith requires God as the sole object of its focus.

By grace, God has given us faith. It is a free gift, which He has bestowed on us. Faith can be directed properly, or it can be misdirected. Three kinds of faith are referred to in the Scriptures:

> Little Faith—that is, selfish faith
>
> Great Faith—that is, selfless faith
>
> Perfect Faith—that is, sacrificial faith

All Christians function in these three levels of faith. The challenge of the Christian life is to develop faith experiences that are of the Great Faith and Perfect Faith quality.

Our next chapter is concerned with one of the forms of communication through which faith is exercised: prayer.

7

Prayer

Introduction

Summary

If I should neglect prayer but for a single day,
I should lose a great deal of the fire of faith.

—*Martin Luther*

7

Prayer

Do you remember Luke's account of Jesus appearing before His disciples in the Upper Room after the Resurrection?

> While they were still talking about this, Jesus himself stood among them and said to them, "Peace be with you."
> They were startled and frightened, thinking they saw a ghost. He said to them, "Why are you troubled, and why do doubts rise in your minds? Look at my hands and my feet. It is I myself! Touch me and see; a ghost does not have flesh and bones, as you see I have."
> When he had said this, he showed them his hands and feet. And while they still did not believe it because of joy and amazement, he asked them, "Do you have anything here to eat?" They gave him a piece of broiled fish, and he took it and ate it in their presence.
> He said to them, "This is what I told you while I was still with you: Everything must be fulfilled that is written about me in the Law of Moses, the Prophets and the Psalms." *(Luke 24:36-44)*

The disciples were wishing Jesus would help them and lead them; when He actually appeared and their prayers were answered, they were startled and disbelieving.

Someone has said, "We pray to our Heavenly Father and live like orphans."

Consider some basic questions:

- Does prayer change God's mind?
- Is it possible that prayer changes you?
- Are long, detailed prayers necessarily a sign of spiritual growth?
- Are you convinced that nothing of real spiritual significance happens to you without a vital prayer life?
- Are you simply eager to know God better and to take time to commune with Him?

Oswald Chambers deals with a principle here that is necessary to understand and embrace if prayer is going to be vital: "Prayer is an on-purpose act . . . a discipline of the body, soul, and spirit." Jesus reflected this same discipline when He said:

> When you pray, go into your room, close the door and pray to your Father, who is unseen. Then your Father, who sees what is done in secret, will reward you.   *(Matt. 6:6)*

Oswald Chambers describes it this way:

> Jesus did not say—Dream about thy Father in secret, but pray to thy Father in secret. Prayer is an effort of the will . . . the most difficult thing to do is to pray: We cannot get our minds into working order, and the first thing that conflicts is wandering thoughts. The great battle in private prayer is the overcoming of mental wool-gathering. We have to discipline our minds and concentrate on willful prayer.[1]

Then Chambers goes on to say:

> It is not part of the life of a natural man to pray. We hear it said that a man will suffer in his life if he does not pray; I question it. What will suffer is the life of the Son of God in him, which is nourished not by food, but by prayer. When a man is born from above, the life of the Son of God is born in him, and he can either starve that life or nourish it. Prayer is the way the life of God is nourished. Our ordinary views of prayer are not found in the New Testament. We look upon prayer as a means of getting things for ourselves; the Bible idea of prayer is that we may get to know God Himself.[2]

E. Stanley Jones describes the heart of the prayer in this manner:

> O, Father, give me the prayerful heart. Let prayers pervade my soul as blood pervades my body. And just as blood carries sustenance and brings away impurities, so let prayer sustain and cleanse me. Amen.[3]

The disciples approached Jesus and said, "Lord, teach us to pray" (Luke 11:1). What benefits are found in learning to wait upon the Lord in prayer! The following three sections are offered to enhance the level of your prayer life:

I. The Fraternity of Prayer

II. The Framework of Prayer

III. The Forms of Prayer

I. The Fraternity of Prayer

The greatest single concept to be learned about prayer is that *prayer is a relationship,* a fellowship, a fraternity with God. Dr. J. G. Morrison was asked: "How much religion does a man need to get to

---

1. Chambers, *My Utmost for His Highest,* 236.
2. Ibid., 241.
3. From *The Way to Power and Poise,* by E. Stanley Jones. Copyright 1949 by Pierce and Smith. Copyright renewal 1977 by Eunice Treffry Matthews. Used by permission of Abingdon Press.

heaven?" He replied, "Just enough to feel comfortable in the presence of the Lord."

From the beginning God created us for the purpose of fellowship. The intimacy of the divine/human relationship develops through the fraternity of prayer.

The fraternity of prayer begins to develop when the following elements are present:

A. Clear Conscience

Beyond the prayer of confession there must be a continual relationship of honesty before God.

You cannot *buy* a clear conscience. A clear conscience cannot be gained through *legislation*. A clear conscience cannot be developed through *environmental shaping*.

There is no way of overestimating the importance of a clear conscience in this matter of prayer; it comes only by obeying the still, small voice of the Holy Spirit.

When you experience a clear conscience as a continual reality in your life, there comes an assurance in your prayer life that nothing else can replace or fully explain.

B. Ask Boldly

Look again at Heb. 4:14-16:

> Therefore, since we have a great high priest who has gone through the heavens, Jesus the Son of God, let us hold firmly to the faith we profess. For we do not have a high priest who is unable to sympathize with our weaknesses, but we have one who has been tempted in every way, just as we are—yet was without sin. Let us then approach the throne of grace with confidence, so that we may receive mercy and find grace to help us in our time of need.

You see, it is only because the blood of Jesus has been applied to your sins that you have the *right* to ask; if you have that right, then *not* to ask boldly is to refuse your God-given privilege.

C. Pray Expecting

> He that cometh to God must believe that he is, and that he is a rewarder of them that diligently seek him.   *(Heb. 11:6, KJV)*

Paul, in Phil. 4:6, says it another way:

> Do not be anxious about anything, but in everything, by prayer and petition, with thanksgiving, present your requests to God.

Of all the New Testament stories of answered prayer, perhaps none explains this principle of *expectation* better than the woman with the issue of blood. Trying to get in to where Jesus was, she was heard saying, "If I could but touch the hem of His garment, I would be healed" (see Matt. 9:20-21, KJV). What boldness that took! What a sense of expectancy!

The fraternity of prayer is step one. Until this relationship is established, prayer will be uncomfortable, unproductive, and even a condemnation.

II. The Framework of Prayer

Webster defines *framework* as "a structure serving to hold the parts of something together or to support something constructed or stretched over or around it."

There is clearly a biblical framework given that will serve to make your prayer life less confusing and more consistent with God's plan.

In order to have a peaceful and productive prayer life in the midst of all the clamoring voices of the "Name It—Claim It" and "Instant Success" theories, you need to rediscover what the Bible says about the framework of prayer.

Dr. Adrian Rogers said, "I'll claim whatever He names."

Certainly, God's children do live far below their privileges. However, the recognition of that failure does not change the Word of God with respect to prayer. Each of us needs to seek more earnestly to pray as *He* directs us to.

There are two considerations in this framework that need to be closely observed and lived by.

A. The Human Framework

For the most part, those who are espousing the "Name It—Claim It" concept of prayer are sincere. However, some, in their attempt to propagate the gospel, have taken advantage of the unsuspecting Christian.

There are several scriptures that have been misused to support this concept, but certainly the most popular is:

> I tell you the truth, if anyone says to this mountain, "Go, throw yourself into the sea," and does not doubt in his heart but believes that what he says will happen, it will be done for him.
> Therefore I tell you, whatever you ask for in prayer, believe that you have received it, and it will be yours. *(Mark 11:23-24)*

There are, among God's children, those who believe that this is a carte blanche to anything they want—health, wealth, or success of any kind. To whatever idea this kind of misuse of Scripture is applied, it is dangerous.

Before committing yourself to the "Name It—Claim It" philosophy, you should take into consideration the following thoughts from Scripture:

1. Since Jesus was standing on the Mount of Olives preaching to both the sinner and the saint, does "anyone" in verse 23 include both? If not, where does it say that?

2. Is there any record that Jesus threw a "mountain . . . into the sea"? Jesus is speaking symbolically rather than literally.

3. Could you imagine any sensitive born-again and Spirit-filled Christian believing for something outside of God's will?

Oswald Chambers says he can't even imagine that a Spirit-filled Christian would think of wanting any other will than God's.

But, you say, is it possible for Christians in their humanness to want something out of God's will? Yes! Humanly, but not in the Spirit. Jesus expressed this same restriction in His model prayer when He said, "Our Father in heaven, hallowed be your name, your kingdom come, *your will* be done on earth as it is in heaven" (Matt. 6:9-10, italics added).

Dr. Adrian Rogers also said, "A prayer that ends in heaven also begins in heaven." In other words, if it carries out God's will, it starts out as God's will.

4. Since all human beings are challenged with the capacity for failure, is it conceivable that they could, on occasion, be wrong in their desires and prayers? The Bible is clear at that point.

> In the same way, the Spirit helps us in our weakness. We do not know what we ought to pray for, but the Spirit himself intercedes for us with groans that words cannot express.   *(Rom. 8:26)*

The human framework of prayer may not be intentionally wrong or contrary to God's will, but whatever the motives, it could be incorrect.

B. God's Framework

Now, consider some examples of prayer that are constructed within the framework of God's will:

1. In Luke 22:39-44, Jesus beautifully portrays, by His life, the profound reality that all prayer must be prayed within the framework of God's will:

> Jesus went out as usual to the Mount of Olives, and his disciples followed him. On reaching the place, he said to them, "Pray that you will not fall into temptation." He withdrew about a stone's throw beyond them, knelt down and prayed, "Father, if you are willing, take this cup from me; yet not my will, but yours be done."
> An angel from heaven appeared to him and strengthened him.

And being in anguish, he prayed more earnestly, and his sweat was like drops of blood falling to the ground.

Jesus clearly desired that He not drink of the cup when He said these words: "Take this cup from me; yet not my will [my desire], but yours." How can anything but God's will, ahead of our human desire, be read into this?

2. In Rom. 8:26-28, Paul deals with this same principle of inability to always know how to pray:

In the same way, the Spirit helps us in our weakness. We do not know what we ought to pray for, but the Spirit himself intercedes for us with groans that words cannot express.

And he who searches our hearts knows the mind of the Spirit, because the Spirit intercedes for the saints in accordance with God's will.

And we know that in all things God works for the good of those who love him, who have been called according to his purpose.

It seems clear that any prayer that is out of the will of God, any prayer that does not depend upon the Spirit's assistance, could be in trouble.

You might think, "If everything must be God's will, why pray?" That, too, is clearly answered in James's Epistle, chapter 4, verse 2:

You want something but don't get it. You kill and covet, but you cannot have what you want. You quarrel and fight. You do not have, because you do not ask God.

Then in verse 3 of this same passage, he emphasizes the point of this treatise:

When you ask, you do not receive, because you ask with wrong motives, that you may spend what you get on your pleasures.

The framework of prayer was designed by God and delivered by God, and it determines both our destiny and rate of spiritual growth. For you to seek answers outside of that framework is to perceive yourself as being wiser than Him.

III. The Forms of Prayer

A. Praise

The prayer of praise is a prayer form that works in both directions—to God and to other believers. Paul, to the church at Philippi, caught the real meaning of praise when he said:

Finally, brothers, whatever is true, whatever is noble, whatever is right, whatever is pure, whatever is lovely, whatever is admirable—if anything is excellent or praiseworthy—think about such things.

(Phil. 4:8)

In other words, though the intent in your prayer of praise is toward God, your own spirit and soul are refreshed and built up as a by-product of your praising Him.

Mary, the mother of Jesus, caught this idea when she said:

> My soul glorifies the Lord and my spirit rejoices in God my Savior, for he has been mindful of the humble state of his servant. From now on all generations will call me blessed, for the Mighty One has done great things for me—holy is his name.   *(Luke 1:46-49)*

There are many tools that you can use to experience this praise form. Here are a few suggestions:

- Meditation on the Word of God, especially many areas in the Psalms

- Meditation on and participation in music, records, tapes, and so on

- Meditating by getting quiet before God

B. Thanksgiving

To express one's deep sense of gratitude for who God is and for what He has done—this is thanksgiving.

Paul caught sight of this in his challenge to the church at Colossae when he said: "So then, just as you received Christ Jesus as Lord, continue to live in him, rooted and built up in him, strengthened in the faith as you were taught, and overflowing with thankfulness" (Col. 2:6).

Someone has said, "Thanksgiving is not thanksgiving until it is expressed."

The classic Bible example of this is recorded in Luke 17:11-19:

> Now on his way to Jerusalem, Jesus traveled along the border between Samaria and Galilee.
> As he was going into a village, ten men who had leprosy met him. They stood at a distance and called out in a loud voice, "Jesus, Master, have pity on us!"
> When he saw them, he said, "Go, show yourselves to the priests." And as they went, they were cleansed.
> One of them, when he saw he was healed, came back, praising God in a loud voice. He threw himself at Jesus' feet and thanked him—and he was a Samaritan.
> Jesus asked, "Were not all ten cleansed? Where are the other nine? Was no one found to return and give praise to God except this foreigner?" Then he said to him, "Rise and go; your faith has made you well."

The essence of this story is that 10 were healed, but only 1 was thankful. It may be true that others of the 9 experienced a feeling of gratitude, but until it is expressed, it is not gratitude in the fullest sense.

One practical way to learn how to practice the prayer of

thanksgiving is to take a few minutes each week and write down not only the ever-present reasons for gratitude but also the particular ones of the week that has just ended.

In the box below, list three things for which you are thankful:

1. _____

2. _____

3. _____

C. Petition

The prayer of petition is asking God to meet your need in some particular sense. Paul expressed it this way in Phil. 4:19:

> And my God will meet all your needs according to his glorious riches in Christ Jesus.

However, petition is more than "asking for things from God"; it is entering into a relationship with Him until when you ask, it is like asking your earthly parent for something, believing that need will be met.

It is vital that you understand that petition (asking God to meet your need) is predicated on the quality of your relationship. One of the reasons many people don't pray as they should is the poor quality of their relationship or fraternity with God.

This is even true of a sinner. David describes the proper attitude of a sinner in Ps. 51:17:

> The sacrifices of God are a broken spirit; a broken and contrite heart, O God, you will not despise.

D. Intercession

Intercessory prayer is the most mature form of prayer. It is the acting or pleading in behalf of someone else.

Consider the following diagram:

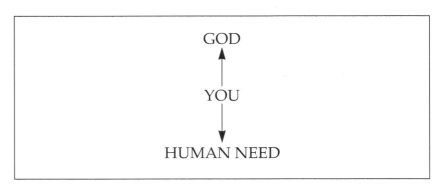

GOD

↑

YOU

↓

HUMAN NEED

This diagram is an attempt to show how you call on God on behalf of someone else. This is intercession.

Intercessory prayer is only effective when there is complete and continual communion with God on behalf of someone else. When a person is willing to be involved in intercessory prayer, he or she will begin to feel the evidence of spiritual growth that is most gratifying.

Therefore, the question is not so much, "How does God answer prayer?" but rather:

- Is my relationship to God such that prayer is as natural as breathing?
- Is my will surrendered to His will in my praying?
- Is my prayer life manifested in all the forms of prayer: praise, thanksgiving, petition, and intercession?

Summary

Prayer is the key element in building our relationship with God. Prayers are a sweet offering to Him. God instructed Moses that the altar of incense was to be kept burning continually in the Tabernacle; the incense represented the prayers of Israel ascending to a covenant-keeping God. In Rev. 5:8 the golden bowls of incense are defined as "the prayers of the saints" (NASB).

Through the fraternity of prayer, we learn to know God better and better. How is this fraternal relationship nurtured? Through the diligent cultivation of a clear conscience and through asking boldly, according to His will. These elements together work to bind our hearts with His.

What is the framework of prayer? One will find great reward in praying in accordance with God's will. In James God instructs us to ask; He wants us to run to Him about all the big and little things that are on our minds. This is how a relationship is built. But He also wants us to seek His will, to discover His plans, and to adopt His point of view concerning our wants and needs.

From a human perspective, though the intent is there, there is sometimes a failure to really ask in accordance with God's will. Sometimes human frailty is so pressed by the enormity of the needs that the believer is unable to discover clearly His will regarding its solution. The Holy Spirit helps us to pray as we ought in such times. These periods of storm and stress are nonetheless important in helping us develop a fraternal relationship with God through prayer.

The richness of one's experience of prayer can be enhanced

when we discover the forms of prayer that are available. The most common forms are these:

> **Praise**—Admiration of God; exulting in His greatness
>
> **Thanksgiving**—Expression of deep gratitude to God for who and what He is
>
> **Petition**—Presentation of needs on our own behalf
>
> **Intercession**—The most mature form of prayer; the presentation of needs on behalf of others

Prayer enhances our relationship with God. It helps us know God better. It puts us in a position to have a more immediate perception of His will. It is to the subject of knowing God's will that we will turn in chapter 8.

8

Knowing God's Will

Introduction

   I. The Plan

     A. Creation Attests to God's Plan

     B. The Word of God Attests to His Plan

        1. There is considerable scriptural evidence that there is a divine plan for each redeemed life.

        2. There are many examples in the Bible of those who chose to *do* God's will.

           a. Old Testament Examples

              (1) David

              (2) Isaiah

              (3) Jeremiah

           b. New Testament Examples

              (1) Jesus

              (2) Paul

  II. The Problem

     A. Rejection

     B. Procrastination

 III. The Procedure

     A. Four Principles

     B. Another Method

Summary

My stubborn will at last hath yielded;
  I would be Thine, and Thine alone.
And this the prayer my lips are bringing:
  "Lord, let in me Thy will be done."
Sweet will of God, still fold me closer,
  Till I am wholly lost in Thee.
Sweet will of God, still fold me closer,
  Till I am wholly lost in Thee.

—*Mrs. C. H. Morris*

8

Knowing God's Will

The subject of God's will is at the very heart of the entire concept of discipling. The fact that God has a wonderful and special plan for your life must be a conviction with you. You must be able to face each set of circumstances throughout life with the confidence, not only that God has a plan, but also that He can be depended on to reveal that plan on a day-to-day basis to all of His children.

From the earliest moments of your Christian life through the most advanced stages of Christian maturity, you will find God's will to be at the crux of every situation. It is upon God's will that all of life pivots. It was Chambers who said, "Faith includes being so convinced of God's plan that you waive all of your personal rights in favor of pursuing His will." Thus, faith is only divine faith when it is centered in God's will. The genuine Christian would not want anything in life that was out of harmony with God's will. Therefore, there is no such thing as divine *faith* that is not grounded in the *will* of God.

For the Christian, the attitude and activity of forever being in intense pursuit of not only *knowing* but also *doing* God's will is not an option but a mandate. In this chapter the subject of God's will is presented in the following manner:

I. The Plan

II. The Problem

III. The Procedure

I. The Plan

Once you come to know Christ in the meaningful experiences of the *new birth* and the *Spirit-filled life,* you will discover that God has a definite purpose and plan for your life.

How many wonderful Christian people do you know who theoretically agree that God has a wonderful plan for their lives, but when being totally honest, admit that they are not really convinced this theory is true? As a result of this uncertainty, they are of little value to themselves or to God's cause.

There is a goal and a course for everyone. Once this vital fact grips the heart, the whole matter of life takes on a new meaning. You see, there can be little enthusiasm in people who are seeking something of which they are not convinced.

The fact that God has a definite plan for your life is abundantly clear in at least two areas:

A. Creation Attests to God's Plan

Think for a moment of the wonderful plan for nature: the flowers, the trees, the animals, the cosmos. If God's intelligence planned that, consider how much more He would plan for His highest handiwork—the human family.

B. The Word of God Attests to His Plan

1. There is considerable scriptural evidence that there is a divine plan for each redeemed life. This fact is supported in scripture taken from both the Old and New Testaments.

Take time to look up and write down the key thought of each: Key Thought
Jer. 29:11 (TLB) _____
Ps. 143:10 (TLB) _____
Isa. 50:4, 7 (TLB) _____
Rom. 12:1-2 _____
Eph. 5:17 _____
Col. 4:12 _____

2. There are many examples in the Bible of those who chose to *do* God's will. Use the examples in the boxes below as additional resource material.

a. Old Testament Examples

(1) David
    Ps. 37:23 (TLB)
    Ps. 139:16 (TLB)
(2) Isaiah
    Isa. 49:1-9 (TLB)
(3) Jeremiah
    Jer. 1:4-10 (TLB)
    Jer. 15:19-21 (TLB)

b. New Testament Examples

(1) Jesus
    John 4:34
    John 6:38
(2) Paul
    Acts 20:24
    2 Tim. 4:7

One of the tragedies in this area is that many people believe at God's will includes only ministers or missionaries. The specific ill of God includes everyone!

The truth is—the following three scriptures present enough in-rmation about God's will to keep us busy.

- It is the will of God that all be saved.

> He is patient with you, not wanting anyone to perish, but every-one to come to repentance. *(2 Pet. 3:9)*

- It is the will of God that all be sanctified.

> For this is the will of God, your sanctification. *(1 Thess. 4:3, NRSV)*

- It is the will of God that all believers carry out the Great Commission.

> Therefore go and make disciples of all nations, baptizing them in the name of the Father and of the Son and of the Holy Spirit, and teaching them to obey everything I have commanded you. And surely I am with you always, to the very end of the age. *(Matt. 28:19-20)*

II. The Problem

God's Word assures you that He has a plan for your life. This is an incredible fact that *is* very clear in His mind and *can be* very clear to you. However, because of your ability to choose, you have the po-tential problem of missing His plan.

It is possible to miss God's plan through either rejection or pro-crastination. Though these responses come from different motives, the objective results are the same.

Let's take a closer look:

A. Rejection

This happens when you completely turn your back on God's will and are ultimately lost. Here is a classical biblical illustration of re-jection:

> Thus Solomon did what was clearly wrong and refused to follow the Lord as his father David did. . . . So now the Lord said to him, "Since you have not kept our agreement and have not obeyed my laws, I will tear the kingdom away from you and your family and give it to someone else." *(1 Kings 11:6, 11, TLB)*

B. Procrastination

To procrastinate may result in your getting into a position where circumstance, age, or condition will not permit you to live out God's perfect will. Consequently, you have to settle for God's per-missive will—His second best.

In both cases, you have missed God's will, even though from different motives.

The following illustration should make this clear:

> What about the person who missed God's will early in life? He or she turned away from God and chose his or her own sinful and selfish way. Later in life, the person comes to God and, out of a genuine, sincere, committed heart and life, consecrates all the rest of life to Christ. Does that mean the person must live a second-rate Christian life? The answer is no—not second-*rate*, but second-*best*.

A person can begin by saying, "Lord, I *want* to obey You. I intend to obey You. But there is no way I can do it right now." If this pattern continues, one will eventually turn his or her back on God.

Suppose at 16 you were called by God into special service, whether as a layperson or minister, but you refused to follow that plan. At the age of 56 you come back to God. There are several losses you have suffered that you must face:

- Forty years of service have been lost.
- Forty years of spiritual growth have been forfeited.
- Scars from your former life of sin will linger long in your functional life, that is, body, soul, and spirit.

The law of retribution is operative regardless of your spiritual relationship with God.

> Do not be deceived: God cannot be mocked. A man reaps what he sows.
>   (Gal. 6:7)

Facing this fact is not meant as a *deterrent* or a discouragement in achieving spiritual excellence in your relationship with God. It is rather an attempt to cause you to *face objectively the results of procrastination or rejection and prod you to WASTE NO TIME in finding and fulfilling God's perfect will for you today.*

III. The Procedure

You may have read accounts of how God has revealed His will to us. Since "God is no respecter of persons" (Acts 10:34, KJV), it shouldn't be too difficult to believe He will do the same for you.

God's Word says:
- He appeared to Abraham in physical form.
- He appeared to Moses in the burning bush.
- He called Samuel by name—in an audible voice.
- He struck Paul down on the road to Damascus.

Most Christians today believe it is no longer necessary for God to perform supernatural physical acts to guide His people, since He has given them His written, Declared, and Living Word. For the most part, your path is clearly spelled out in His Word.

A. Four Principles

One way of knowing God's will for your life is to consider it in the light of these four principles:

1. Remember that God's plan is very clear to Him. A classic illustration of this is Jesus in Gethsemane. Even though *Jesus* struggled with God's will, it was always there.

> He withdrew about a stone's throw beyond them, knelt down and prayed, "Father, *if you are willing, take this cup from me; yet not my will, but yours be done.*"   (Luke 22:41-42, *italics added*)

It was the voice of human agony that cried out. Jesus would not have been human if He had not been affected by this struggle. The Son of God, oppressed by His greatest test, had to fight His way through this temptation to see and accept God's will.

2. To find God's will does not mean that you must set aside your own God-given abilities. The thrilling thing is that many times God uses our natural functions, that is, heart and soul, to reveal His plan. These functions must always be yielded and responsive to His will.

> In the same way, count yourselves dead to sin but alive to God in Christ Jesus. Therefore do not let sin reign in your mortal body so that you obey its evil desires. Do not offer the parts of your body to sin, as instruments of wickedness, but rather offer yourselves to God, as those who have been brought from death to life; and offer the parts of your body to him as instruments of righteousness.   (Rom. 6:11-13)

3. The use of the Scriptures in knowing God's will may be twofold:

a. God may give you the light you seek by a verse. But even this has dangers that must be avoided, because you may find a scripture that fits your will but which may not be God's will.

b. Second, the scripture that seems to prove your desire should be weighed along with circumstances.

4. However, the idea that God's will cannot be something that you desire is biblically untrue. If you are "crucified with Christ" (Gal. 2:20) and have His mind in you, you are so close to His thinking and so under the control of His Spirit that you will seldom even *want* anything that is *not* His will.

> The spiritual man makes judgments about all things, but he himself is not subject to any man's judgment: "For who has known the mind of the Lord that he may instruct him?" But *we have the mind of Christ.*   (1 Cor. 2:15-16, *italics added*)

List three experiences where God has revealed His will to you:

1. _____

2. _____

3. _____

B. Another Method

When there is difficulty in determining God's will in your life, and you are not able to find any clearly written answer from the Word, nor are there any unusual impressions given to you by God, you may want to try the following method that has worked successfully in the lives of many.

A Method to Determine God's Will

1. *Absolute honesty* in wanting God's will.
2. Choose what seems *right* and most fulfilling.
3. Depend upon the *check* of the Holy Spirit.

---

1. Absolute Honesty in Wanting God's Will

Look into your own heart and ask yourself: "Do I want *God's will at any cost?*" Absolute honesty is essential at this point. Unless your pursuit of God's will is *motivated by a pure, unmixed motive,* you do not have an adequate foundation upon which to build a direction or a decision.

Just as the foundation of a building is an absolute *must* to insure the function, security, and beauty of that building, so is unquestioned honesty in wanting God's will a *must* if you are to know and experience His will in your life.

2. Choose What Seems Right and Most Fulfilling

If either through *your spirit* or *God's Word* you cannot discern God's will, then *you must use your own spiritual and psychological judgment* to *choose what seems to be the right* thing for you to do.

Many times God's will is exactly what you want for yourself *because you have the mind of Christ in you.* When you are *absolutely honest* and *unmixed in your motive,* God's *unrevealed will and your will* are *often the same.*

The paraphrase of John 14:22-24 in *The Living Bible* speaks clearly to this principle:

> Judas (not Judas Iscariot, but his other disciple with that name) said to him, "Sir, why are you going to reveal yourself only to us disciples and not to the world at large?" Jesus replied, "Because I will only reveal myself to those who love me and obey me. The Father will love them too, and we will come to them and live with them. Anyone who doesn't obey me doesn't love me. And remember, I am not making up this answer to your question! It is the answer given by the Father who sent me."

When determining direction, a good rule to remember is that never does God's will conflict with the *Scriptures.* As you are praying and pursuing God's direction, be *careful* that it does not conflict with the Word of God. When you are making a decision about the right and most fulfilling thing to do, *know that God's will never conflicts with His Word.*

3. Depend upon the Check of the Holy Spirit

Look at this step-by-step procedure:

a. Now that you are sure that you want God's will at any cost, and

b. Now that you have chosen what seems to be the right and most fulfilling thing to do,

c. Now you can depend on the faithful Holy Spirit to check you if you are wrong or to assure you if you are right.

Look at John 7:17:

> If any man will *do* his will, he shall *know* of the doctrine, *whether it be of God*, or whether I speak of myself.   (KJV, *italics added*)

The principle of this verse is that *if your motive is pure and you want only God's will, He will guide you,* and *you will know whether it is of God or of self.* If your decision is wrong, you will sense a heaviness or an uneasiness come over you. If you are right, you will sense an assurance.

Therefore, when the will of God is not one of those clearly written or discerned utterances in your life, there is a very *sure method of receiving God's guidance.*

Without looking back, list the three steps in this method of knowing God's will:

1. _____

2. _____

3. _____

4. One Final Thought

If for some fault of human perception you have not been sensitive enough to see or feel the clouds of uneasiness, and as a result you *do* make a mistake, this you can count on:

a. Because of your integrity and pure motive, and

b. Because of the character of God,

He will keep you and work out the situation for your best.

Summary

In the life of most believers there is little problem with *doing* God's will. Most Christians would gladly *do* His will if they only knew what it was He wanted them to do. *Knowing* God's will is the central issue. How can you know God's will?

First of all, we should take consolation in knowing that *He knows what His will is for us.* It is very plain to Him. Second, He wants us to know His plan for us. Third, He wants us to follow His plan.

It is also important that we keep before ourselves the fact that we can miss His plan. How? Through outright refusal to accept His Lordship and leadership in our lives and by procrastinating. When God shows us something to do, He wants us to do it. Procrastination can be a subtle form of rebellion; it can be a way of sabotaging His plan by postponing our response.

How can His will be discerned, then? Through immediate forthright obedience. The formula the Scripture offers is: "If you will *do,* you will *know.*" When we respond in obedience to His will, He reveals to us another part of His plan for us.

Another method of determining God's will is the three-step approach:

1. Be certain that you possess absolute honesty in wanting God's will.

2. Choose the alternative that seems to be right and most fulfilling.

3. Depend upon the Holy Spirit to check you if you have chosen wrongly.

Once you have discerned His will, you will tend to respond with an immediacy of commitment to that will. Commitment is a declaration of faith. Chapter 9 is given to the study of commitment.

9

Commitment

Introduction

Summary

Commitment of the total self to God is more
than discipline—it is a matter of worship.

9

Commitment

Commitment is a word that is so misused and overused that one is hesitant to use it. It is important that we understand *commitment* correctly and resolve to live it out consistently.

For the use of this study, *commitment* will be defined as "an act of entrusting something or someone to another." What is entrusted to you is to be used for the purpose for which it was given. So whether from God to you or you to God, what is committed should be used for the purpose for which the gift was intended.

In chapter 1, "Mandate of the Master," it was learned that a disciple is a person who is committed to Christ in obedience and service. This study will center around two questions—"What Did God Commit to Humankind?" and "What Should You Commit to God?"

I. What Did God Commit to Humankind?

In Gen. 1:26 through 2:3, there is the record of what God has committed to humankind:

> Then God said, "Let us make man in our image, in our likeness, and let them rule over the fish of the sea and the birds of the air, over the livestock, over all the earth, and over all the creatures that move along the ground."
>
> So God created man in his own image, in the image of God he created him; male and female he created them.
>
> God blessed them and said to them, "Be fruitful and increase in number; fill the earth and subdue it. Rule over the fish of the sea and the birds of the air and over every living creature that moves on the ground."
>
> Then God said, "I give you every seed-bearing plant on the face of the whole earth and every tree that has fruit with seed in it. They will be yours for food. And to all the beasts of the earth and all the birds of the air and all the creatures that move on the ground—everything that has the breath of life in it—I give every green plant for food." And it was so.
>
> God saw all that he had made, and it was very good. And there was evening, and there was morning—the sixth day.
>
> Thus the heavens and the earth were completed in all their vast array.
>
> By the seventh day God had finished the work he had been doing; so on the seventh day he rested from all his work. And God

blessed the seventh day and made it holy, because on it he rested from all the work of creating that he had done.

Specifically, God committed these three things to human beings:

A. Personhood—like Himself

"Let us make [create] man in our own image, in our likeness."

1. Physical Life

If we are created in His likeness, it is obvious that God has some kind of essence that can be identified.

> Then the man and his wife heard the sound of the LORD God as he was walking in the garden in the cool of the day, and they hid from the LORD God among the trees of the garden.　　*(Gen. 3:8)*

However, our physical body was created in a temporal form, while God's essence is spiritual or eternal in nature.

2. Psychical Life

This psychical function of human beings is the nonmaterial portion of the physical body; it is identifiable by intelligence, emotions, and will.

3. Spiritual Life

The Spirit of God is the divine Agent that brought *order* out of *chaos.* The only biblically orthodox theology is one that is based on a valid doctrine of creation.

In each person, this same intelligent, emotional, and volitional spirit—when it is cleansed by the Holy Spirit—can bring *order* out of spiritual *chaos.*

So the personhood that God committed to us is in the likeness of a personal, intelligent, and holy God.

B. The Rulership of His Creation

> ". . . and let them rule over the fish of the sea and the birds of the air, over the livestock, over all the earth, and over all the creatures that move along the ground."
>
> So God created man in his own image, in the image of God he created him; male and female he created them.
>
> God blessed them and said to them, "Be fruitful and increase in number; fill the earth and subdue it. Rule over the fish of the sea and the birds of the air and over every living creature that moves on the ground."
>
> Then God said, "I give you every seed-bearing plant on the face of the whole earth and every tree that has fruit with seed in it. They will be yours for food. And to all the beasts of the earth and all the birds of the air and all the creatures that move on the ground—everything that has the breath of life in it—I give every green plant for food." And it was so.
>
> God saw all that he had made, and it was very good. And there was evening, and there was morning—the sixth day.　　*(Gen. 1:26-31)*

Did you ever stop to ask yourself, what else could we want

that God didn't commit to us? God has provided us with every conceivable thing to make us happy.

C. The Capacity to Worship Him

Having been created in His image, with intelligence, emotion, and volition, we have the capacity to worship God with understanding, feeling, and free choice. None other of God's creation has this capacity.

Exod. 20:1-6 speaks clearly of God's desire that all worship Him only:

> And God spoke all these words:
> "I am the LORD your God, who brought you out of Egypt, out of the land of slavery.
> "You shall have no other gods before me.
> "You shall not make for yourself an idol in the form of anything in heaven above or on the earth beneath or in the waters below. You shall not bow down to them or worship them; for I, the LORD your God, am a jealous God, punishing the children for the sin of the fathers to the third and fourth generation of those who hate me, but showing love to a thousand generations of those who love me and keep my commandments."

II. What Should You Commit to God?

The key to this question turns on the answers to the following questions:

• Do you see yourself as an owner of what you possess or as a steward of what you possess?

• Is your attitude toward what you possess one of gratitude, or is it one of deserving what you have?

In light of these questions, look again at the main question, "What should you commit to God?"

A. Commit Your Personhood

Paul, in his first letter to the Thessalonians, chapter 5, verse 23, clearly exhorts us to commit our self to God:

> May your whole spirit, soul and body be kept blameless at the coming of our Lord Jesus Christ.

In Rom. 12:1-2, Paul describes that commitment this way:

> Therefore, I urge you, brothers, in view of God's mercy, to offer your bodies as living sacrifices, holy and pleasing to God—this is your spiritual act of worship.
> Do not conform any longer to the pattern of this world, but be transformed by the renewing of your mind. Then you will be able to test and approve what God's will is—his good, pleasing and perfect will.

It is evident in God's Word, and specifically by these two scriptures, that commitment of the total self to God is more than discipline—it is a matter of worship. Paul said, "This is your spiritual act of worship."

This elevates the care of the body, soul, and spirit above mere vanity. Apply the following three scriptures to this principle of spiritual worship:

1. Care of the Body, 1 Cor. 3:16

> Don't you know that you yourselves are God's temple and that God's Spirit lives in you?

Taking care of one's body can be an expression of commitment to God.

2. Care of the Soul, Phil. 4:8-9

> Finally, brothers, whatever is true, whatever is noble, whatever is right, whatever is pure, whatever is lovely, whatever is admirable—if anything is excellent or praiseworthy—*think* about such things.
> Whatever you have learned or received or heard from me, or seen in me—put it into practice. And the God of peace will be with you.
> *(italics added)*

The psychical function of mind, emotions, and will must also be committed to God.

As you studied in chapter 3 of this book, the psychical function is imperfectible in this life; nonetheless it is capable of being better balanced and more under the control of the Holy Spirit.

Paul referred to this when he said,

> But *I keep under my body,* and *bring it into subjection:* lest that by any means, when I have preached to others, I myself should be a castaway.   *(1 Cor. 9:27, KJV, italics added)*

This is a daily commitment and discipline of the amoral function of both the material portion of the human nature (the body) and the immaterial portion of the human nature (the soul).

When the mind and will master the body, there begins to emerge a psychical peace that is not attainable any other way.

3. Care of the Spirit, Prov. 3:5

> Trust in the LORD with all your *heart* and lean not on your own understanding.   *(italics added)*

In this passage of Scripture the wise man Solomon declares that if you will commit your heart to God, "He will make your paths straight" (v. 6).

So the commitment we make to God is an exciting experience that is not only attainable in this life but also one that every sincere Christian wants to make.

Take a moment right now to close out the surrounding world and make that commitment of yourself—body, soul, and spirit—to God.

If your commitment has been complete, the influence of your life will be felt in the lives of those about you; your influence will reflect this commitment.

There is no asset that the committed Christian possesses that will affect this world like a full commitment of himself or herself to God.

B. Commit Your Possessions

You may be tempted to think that your possessions are small and insignificant. Though some of your possessions may be smaller than those of someone else, another part of your possessions is exactly the same.

1. Time

"Commitment of your total self" includes giving back to God the time that He has given to you.

Is there any way to correctly put a value on this gift? Time is that space in life in which to do and to become the will of God.

There is a sense in which everyone has the same 24 hours in a day. The question is, "Is your time committed to God? Are you using it in a way that pleases Him, prepares you, and presents your ministry to a needy world?"

> List four ways you could better commit your time to carry out God's will:
>
> 1. _____
> 2. _____
> 3. _____
> 4. _____

2. Talents

You have active as well as latent talents, abilities, and gifts with which God has entrusted you. There are three distinct things about these talents you need to consider:

a. You need to discover prayerfully what these talents are. It is important that you understand your awesome responsibility here.

Rom. 12 and 1 Cor. 12 display many of the gifts or talents God has bestowed on man. Look at them, explore them, and discover which of them you may possess.

b. Life is a continual experience of cultivating these talents that they may become more effectively used in the work of ministry. Unless this is consciously done, the moral responsibility for that failure lies at your feet.

c. As these talents and gifts are discovered and developed, they need to be dedicated immediately and continually to the work of ministry.

Refusing to develop them will bring clouds of despair and ultimately the guilt of disobedience.

In the following boxes, list the talents you have discovered in recent months and the way you intend to develop them.

Talents You Have Discovered
1. _____
2. _____
3. _____

How You Intend to Develop Them
1. _____
2. _____
3. _____

You may be tempted to think that you have no talents. Decide today to begin searching for your God-given talents. This is God's will for you.

3. Treasure

Someone has said, "Your greatest asset is your attitude or spirit." There is no area in life where this is better reflected than in the matter of your treasures.

Jesus said, in Matt. 6:21, "For where your treasure is, there your heart will be also."

Of Christ's 38 parables, 16 of them refer to our attitude toward money.

There are some principles in Mal. 3:6-12 you need to look at closely:

> "I the LORD do not change. So you, O descendants of Jacob, are not destroyed. Ever since the time of your forefathers you have turned away from my decrees and have not kept them. Return to me, and I will return to you," says the LORD Almighty.
> "But you ask, 'How are we to return?'
> "Will a man rob God? Yet you rob me.
> "But you ask, 'How do we rob you?'
> "In tithes and offerings. You are under a curse—the whole nation of you—because you are robbing me. Bring the whole tithe into the storehouse, that there may be food in my house. Test me in this," says the LORD Almighty, "and see if I will not throw open the floodgates of

heaven and pour out so much blessing that you will not have room enough for it. I will prevent pests from devouring your crops, and the vines in your fields will not cast their fruit," says the LORD Almighty. "Then all the nations will call you blessed, for yours will be a delightful land," says the LORD Almighty.

Look at some of the principles in this passage that warrant serious discussion:

a. V. 6

"I the LORD do not change."

Therefore God's Word is applicable today.

b. V. 7

"Return to me, and I will return to you."

If you are sluggish or disobedient in this area, the answer is clear: You will suffer.

c. V. 8

"'How do we rob you?' In tithes and offerings."

In Exodus chapter 20 God says, "Thou shalt not steal" (v. 15, KJV). This is clearly God's commandment. To violate this is to be under His curse.

d. V. 10

"Bring the whole tithe."

The Hebrew word for *tithe* means 10 percent of your total increase.

e. V. 10

"Bring the whole tithe into the storehouse."

There is no way you can twist this into *not* meaning the church.

f. Vv. 10-12

"Test me in this," says the LORD Almighty, "and see if I will not . . ."

(1) ". . . throw open the floodgates of heaven and pour out so much blessing that you will not have room enough for it."—Spiritual!

(2) "I will prevent pests from devouring your crops, and the vines in your fields will not cast their fruit."—Material!

(3) "Then all the nations will call you blessed, for yours will be a delightful land."—Social!

In all of these references, the bottom line is: "Do you consider yourself an owner or trustee?" The answer to this will reveal your attitude. Your attitude will produce a life of either gratitude or greed.

Because of the character of God, you know that His commitment to you is complete. Such scriptures as the following speak of His complete commitment to you:

While we were still sinners, Christ died for us.　　*(Rom. 5:8)*

For God so loved the world that he gave his one and only Son.

(John 3:16)

Now, in light of His commitment to you, can you afford to do less than commit your all to Him?

In the boxes below, please indicate:

> What has God given you that you have not fully committed to Him?
>
> 1. _____
> 2. _____
> 3. _____
> 4. _____

> What are you willing to do about it?
>
> 1. _____
> 2. _____
> 3. _____
> 4. _____

Summary

In the beginning, at the time of creation, God committed to humankind three things: personhood, rulership of His creation, and the capacity to worship Him. God created us like himself, persons with physical, psychical, and spiritual functions. He committed to us the responsibility to manage the rest of nature well. He also committed to us the capacity to worship Him; in the giving of the Ten Commandments He made it clear that He jealously desires to be the Object of that worship.

In response to God's commitments, we should commit to God our personhood: body, soul, and spirit. When we truly love the Lord with heart, mind, soul, and strength, we are committing our personhood to God. Also, the believer should commit possessions—time, talent, and treasure—to God. Properly understood, we are not the *owner* but the *manager*—the steward—of these possessions.

When we respond to God by committing back to Him the gifts with which we have been entrusted, we please Him. Such commitment is in the truest sense worship; we are fulfilling the purpose for which we were created.

The believer who is committed to God with heart, mind, soul, and strength will find little difficulty in living a life of obedience to His Spirit. Obedience will be the focus of our attention in chapter 10.

10

Obedience

Introduction

Summary

Obey: To be obedient to—execute the commands of; to be ruled or controlled by; to follow restraint, control, or command.

—*Webster*

10

Obedience

The matter of obedience involves all of us in every aspect of our lives. From Genesis to Revelation, God addresses this subject in all kinds of situations.

In the Book of Genesis, God demands obedience from Adam and Eve in order to protect them from the tree of death:

> The LORD God took the man and put him in the Garden of Eden to work it and take care of it. And the LORD God commanded the man, "You are free to eat from any tree in the garden; but you must not eat from the tree of the knowledge of good and evil, for when you eat of it you will surely die."   *(Gen. 2:15-17)*

In the Book of Revelation, we find the path of obedience leading to the tree of life:

> Blessed are those who wash their robes, that they may have the right to the tree of life and may go through the gates into the city.   *(Rev. 22:14)*

This chapter is written to help you become an effective Christian and enjoy the fruits of your obedience.

I. Portraits of Obedience

From the beginning of time, God's one condition has been obedience. Second Chron. 26:5 says, "As long as he [Uzziah] sought the LORD, God gave him success."

There is a tendency within most people to think that these biblical characters were different from us, or that they were specially equipped for this kind of obedience. But the truth is, they were not. They were just like people today.

As you read the following four portraits, fill in the details and relate them to yourself.

A. Noah

In Gen. 6:13-21, God commanded Noah to perform an absolutely unreasonable task. Noah's obedient response was almost bizarre.

Who could imagine someone building, in the front lawn, a ship 450 feet long (that's about one block long), 75 feet wide, and 45 feet high—and it had never rained before!

Who could imagine putting one's entire family, belongings, animals, and fowl on this ship to wait for a flood that had never happened before?

Who could imagine someone enduring all the criticism of an entire region for many years in order to carry out what he believed to be God's will?

The key thought, recorded four different ways in this account of Noah's obedience, is "Noah did everything just as God commanded him" (6:22).

B. Abraham

There is no question that Abraham was God's friend. In the following scripture, Abraham is talking with the angel of the Lord. Let's listen in:

> When Abram was ninety-nine years old, the LORD appeared to him and said, "I am God Almighty; walk before me and be blameless. I will confirm my covenant between me and you and will greatly increase your numbers."
>
> Abram fell facedown, and God said to him, "As for me, this is my covenant with you: You will be the father of many nations. No longer will you be called Abram; your name will be Abraham, for I have made you a father of many nations. I will make you very fruitful; I will make nations of you, and kings will come from you. I will establish my covenant as an everlasting covenant between me and you and your descendants after you for the generations to come, to be your God and the God of your descendants after you. The whole land of Canaan, where you are now an alien, I will give as an everlasting possession to you and your descendants after you; and I will be their God."
>
> Then God said to Abraham, "As for you, you must keep my covenant, you and your descendants after you for the generations to come." *(Gen. 17:1-9)*

God kept His promise by giving Abraham a son. Isaac was born of Sarah, when she was beyond the years of childbearing. This son was God's posterity promise.

Can you imagine the quality of relationship God and Abraham must have established across those years? And then God gave Abraham a most difficult task through which to test his obedience.

> Take your son, your only son, Isaac, whom you love, and go to the region of Moriah. Sacrifice him there as a burnt offering on one of the mountains I will tell you about. *(Gen. 22:2)*

Oswald Chambers, in commenting on this, said:

> God's command is—Take now, not presently. It is extraordinary how we debate! We know a thing is right, but we try to find excuses for not doing it at once. To climb to the height God shows can never be

done presently, it must be done now. The sacrifice is gone through in will before it is performed actually.

"And Abraham *rose up early* in the morning . . . and went into the place of which God had told him" (verse 3). The wonderful simplicity of Abraham! When God spoke, he did not confer with flesh and blood. Beware when you want to confer with flesh and blood, i.e., your own sympathies, your own insight, anything that is not based on your personal relationship to God. These are the things that compete with and hinder obedience to God.[1]

James, the brother of Jesus, in describing this same truth, said that "Abraham's faith was made perfect by what he did" (see James 2:22).

But what did he do?

Abraham took the wood for the burnt offering and placed it on his son Isaac, and he himself carried the fire and the knife. As the two of them went on together, Isaac spoke up and said to his father Abraham, "Father?" "Yes, my son?" Abraham replied. "The fire and wood are here," Isaac said, "but where is the lamb for the burnt offering?" Abraham answered, "God himself will provide the lamb for the burnt offering, my son." And the two of them went on together.

When they reached the place God had told him about, Abraham built an altar there and arranged the wood on it. He bound his son Isaac and laid him on the altar, on top of the wood. Then he reached out his hand and took the knife to slay his son. But the angel of the LORD called out to him from heaven, "Abraham! Abraham!"

"Here I am," he replied. "Do not lay a hand on the boy," he said. "Do not do anything to him. Now I know that you fear God, because you have not withheld from me your son, your only son."

Abraham looked up and there in a thicket he saw a ram caught by its horns. He went over and took the ram and sacrificed it as a burnt offering instead of his son. So Abraham called that place The LORD Will Provide. And to this day it is said, "On the mountain of the LORD it will be provided."

The angel of the LORD called to Abraham from heaven a second time and said, "I swear by myself, declares the LORD, that because you have done this and have not withheld your son, your only son, I will surely bless you and make your descendants as numerous as the stars in the sky and as the sand on the seashore. Your descendants will take possession of the cities of their enemies, and through your offspring all nations on earth will be blessed, because you have obeyed me."

(Gen. 22:6-18)

C. Hannah

This is the woman who was willing to give her only son to God that He might work His plan through the boy who grew up to be the great and fearless prophet of obedience—Samuel.

It's one thing to tell the weak and insignificant how and what you feel, but Samuel, without hesitation, told King Saul:

Does the LORD delight in burnt offerings and sacrifices as much as

---

1. Chambers, *My Utmost for His Highest*, 316.

in obeying the voice of the LORD? To obey is better than sacrifice, and to heed is better than the fat of rams.

For rebellion is like the sin of divination, and arrogance like the evil of idolatry. Because you have rejected the word of the LORD, he has rejected you as king.   *(1 Sam. 15:22-23)*

Thank God for parents who not only are willing to count the cost in honoring God but also are willing to build into their children a quality of character that serves to aid them in paying that price.

D. Jesus Christ

The writer to the Hebrews presents the role of Jesus' obedience in making complete the work of redemption:

Although he was a son, he learned obedience from what he suffered and, once made perfect, he became the source of eternal salvation for all who obey him.   *(5:8-9)*

In His great high-priestly prayer, Jesus offers His obedience to the Father as a worthy sacrifice.

I have brought you glory on earth by completing the work you gave me to do.   *(John 17:4)*

Sometimes people find it difficult to accept that Jesus had to learn obedience just as we do, but it is true. Remember, Jesus was human, just as we are. The Gospels present Jesus, our Brother, as One who walked faithfully in obedience to the Father.

II. Problems with Obedience

If you will take time to discuss the following problem situations and relate them to where you are spiritually, you will better understand the value of immediate obedience.

A.

I don't know God's will for my life. Therefore, it is not *possible* for me to obey, because I'm not *responsible* for what I don't know.

B.

I would rather *dictate* to God and then ask Him to bless my obedience to *my own* will. "Bless my mess!"

C.

I have a problem obeying because of what I think it will *cost others* around me. As an example, my obedience to God may appear to work a hardship on my family.

    NOTE: Someone has said: "God holds himself responsible for the consequences of my obedience."

D.

I believe in "progressive obedience"; I also believe that obedience is optional. I choose to wait and obey fully—next time.

III. Principles of Obedience

You have examined some examples of obedience in the past. Now, let's explore some principles that will help you live out this obedience in your everyday life.

A. The Love Principle

In the last of the Gospels, Jesus discloses this love principle:

> The one who obeys me is the one who loves me; and because he loves me, my Father will love him; and I will too, and I will reveal myself to him.
>   *(John 14:21, TLB)*

For Christians obedience is the language of love. It is how we convey to God our love for Him. Look at this love principle in light of the threefold functional view:

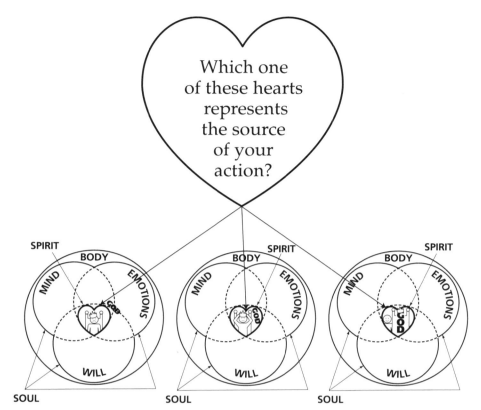

NATURAL/SINFUL MOTIVE   **MIXED MOTIVE**   **PURE MOTIVE**

So the principle simply is: "If you love Me, you will obey Me; and if you obey Me, I will reveal myself to you."

The question is: "Do you really love Him?"

B. The Confidence Principle

Hannah Whitall Smith, in her book *The Christian's Secret of a Happy Life*, reveals a surprising insight: Obedience is the path to happiness! But whether or not we are fixed on that path depends upon where we are placing our confidence.

"Perfect obedience would be perfect happiness if only we had perfect confidence in the power that we were obeying."[2]

The confidence principle more simply stated is: "Perfect obedience is perfect happiness if you have perfect confidence in the One you obey."

---

2. Hannah Whitall Smith, *The Christian's Secret of a Happy Life* (Old Tappan, N.J.: Fleming H. Revell Co., 1952), 208.

This confidence comes when you are so convinced of God's person and purpose that you waive all of your own personal rights in favor of His will for you.

James presents Abraham as a model of faithful obedience:

> You foolish man, do you want evidence that faith without deeds is useless? Was not our ancestor Abraham considered righteous for what he did when he offered his son Isaac on the altar? You see that his faith and his actions were working together, and his faith was made complete by what he did. And the scripture was fulfilled that says, "Abraham believed God, and it was credited to him as righteousness," and he was called God's friend. You see that a person is justified by what he does and not by faith alone. *(James 2:20-24)*

So, when you have confidence in God's will for your life, followed by perfect obedience in carrying out that will, the bottom line is real happiness!

To clarify: This confidence principle is not a psychical confidence, for that is never perfect. It is, rather, a spiritual confidence—a confidence of the spirit.

This confidence of our spirit in the trustworthiness of God is given voice by the psalmist:

> Blessed is the man who does not walk in the counsel of the wicked or stand in the way of sinners or sit in the seat of mockers.
> But his *delight* is in the law of the LORD, and on his law he meditates day and night. *(Ps. 1:1-2, italics added)*

C. The Insight, Opportunity, and Response Principle

In order to appreciate more clearly and practically this principle, look at the following diagram:

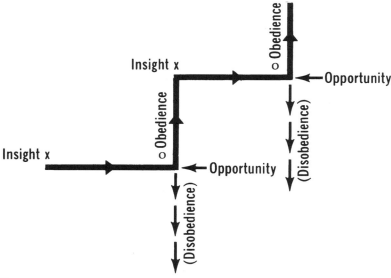

Key:

x—Represents your understanding of God's will for you.

■■—The horizontal lines represent the different lengths of time between God's revelation of His will and when you decide to act upon it.

o— Represents your response. Either it is an affirmative response or a negative response.

This model graphically portrays the dynamics of obedience. Here are four observations worth noting:

1. In this principle, it is simply a matter of obedience or disobedience.

2. God isn't obligated to give you a second insight until you obey the first one.

3. You can grow as rapidly as you want. If you will only obey the insight that you have at the moment, you can move on to new revelations from God.

4. It is highly important that you stay sensitive to God's timing. Obedience does not always follow insight immediately. However, to be insensitive to His timing and miss it is a serious state for any Christian.

The diagram below is another attempt to show that, as you respond positively in your heart to the will of God, it also affects your psychical and physical functions:

God holds himself responsible for the consequences of your obedience, but the reverse of that is also true. When you willfully say no to God's will (insight), you are electing to assume the consequences.

The fear of the LORD is the beginning of wisdom; all who follow
his precepts have good understanding. To him belongs eternal praise.
(Ps. 111:10)

D. The Lag-Time Principle

Now that you have briefly looked at the Love Principle, the Confidence Principle, and the Insight, Opportunity, and Response Principle, you are ready to learn one of the most exciting principles in all of Christian growth! It is called the Lag-Time Principle.

This principle deals with one of the most subtle weapons that Satan can use against you. Through confusion or cleverness, you may not see it as lag-time, but it is.

Dr. Russell V. DeLong used to describe lag-time in decision making as "putting it in the pigeonhole of suspended judgment." The tragedy is that when you know something is God's will and you hesitate to carry it out, the consequences are dangerous and damaging.

There are several things you must clearly understand if you are to use this principle advantageously:

1. Lag-time is that period of time between the moment God reveals His will and the time that elapses before you carry out that will.

2. If in your heart you say no to His will, it is no longer lag-time; it is disobedience.

3. The cause of lag-time is twofold:

a. It is often caused by psychical insecurity, inferiority, or a sense of failure. Such lag-time is the result of human weakness.

b. It can also be caused by the fleshly conflict that exists in the heart of the unsanctified or non-Spirit-filled Christian.

4. Whatever the cause, if you miss God's timing in any situation, the cost is the same. If God wants you to do something for Him and you want to, but, for either human or fleshly reasons, you hesitate and miss His perfect timing, the results are the same.

It is obvious that the devil would like to prolong this period called lag-time. However, sensitive Christians who want God's best strive to reduce this period to the point that they seldom miss God's perfect will.

There are several incidents in the Bible where God's people have suffered from lag-time.

> Take time to read and discuss
> Numbers 13—14.

A poorly maintained devotional life will always result in postponed response. If you think you can afford the luxury of delayed or postponed obedience, then you may as well count on spending the rest of your life stumbling around in spiritual fog.

The person who chronically complains of the malady of "non-revelation" ("I don't know God's will") not only has disclosed a symptom but also has, in the same breath, identified the cause. If you don't know God's will, it's more than likely due to a delinquent response of obedience to His last revelation.

Thus, the growing, dynamic Christian is one who lives in an eager pursuit to carry out all that he or she knows of God's will.

Summary

Obedience is the language of love. Jesus told His followers that if they loved Him, they would obey Him (John 14:21; 15:9-10). Obedience is an observable statement of commitment to Him; obedience is possible because we have chosen to lay aside our own rights of self-rule and have elected to choose what He chooses for us.

In determining to live a life of obedience, we are not without credible models: Noah, Abraham, Hannah, and our Lord himself each provide examples of how obedience becomes enfleshed.

Our level of willingness to obey is often a reflection of where we are placing our confidence. Hannah Whitall Smith said, "Perfect obedience would be perfect happiness if only we had perfect confidence in the power that we were obeying." The confidence level to which she refers is a spiritual confidence.

Obedience is more than a reflective quality; it does more than just identify the epicenter of our spiritual confidence: it also facilitates spiritual growth. This is the principle of insight, opportunity, and obedient response. God isn't obligated to give you a second insight into spiritual principles until you have obeyed the first one He gave. When you do respond in a timely manner, a new insight is given, along with an opportunity to obey Him in the light of that new insight. This is the path of spiritual growth. Progress in spiritual growth is frequently hindered by the principle of lag-time; this is the amount of time that lapses between the point at which you know God's will and the point at which you obey God's will.

As we make progress in curbing the amount of lag-time in our obedience, we become more astute in our ability to discern God's will. A by-product of this is that we will be able to avoid confusion in discovering how we should be spending our time and energies. This subject is treated more fully in chapter 11, "The Priorities of the Christian Life."

II

The Priorities
of the Christian Life

Introduction

Summary

But seek first His kingdom and His righteousness; and all these things shall be added to you.

Matt. 6:33, NASB

II

The Priorities of the Christian Life

Priority: The state of being prior to something else;
      precedence in timing.

—*Webster*

There is no way a non-Christian can fully understand the significance of Christian priorities. The non-Christian value system is different from that of the Christian's; therefore, what is important to the Christian could be, and often is, unimportant to the non-Christian.

Jesus' summary statement on priorities is probably the most frequently quoted by Christians on the subject:

Seek ye first the kingdom of God, and his righteousness.
                                    (Matt. 6:33, KJV)

Nonetheless, even among Christians, the question of priorities poses some knotty problems:

● Establishing priorities is a *pervasive problem.* It involves your assessments—and it involves your relationship with the Church, the Body of Believers. It continually affects your life's perspective and production.

● Establishing priorities is a *personal problem.* Many churches today are on the decline. God is not prejudiced; since He wants His Church to grow, the responsibility for the decline cannot be assigned to His account. The responsibility must rest, in part, with the priority system of individual church members as well as the Church itself.

You have heard many good, intelligent people present plans

for how to prioritize things in your life. They have made lists for you to live by, such as the following:

1. God 2. Home 3. Work 4. Church	1. God 2. Church 3. Home	1. God 2. Home 3. Church 4. Recreation

Even the clergy has been guilty of making a static list of priorities in order to support its philosophical position of ministry. Some would say, "If you have good homes, you will have good churches." This isn't always true.

There is a clear and understandable priority program presented in God's Word. Before looking at it, check your spiritual barometer. Are you willing to take God's plan regarding your priorities?

For the Christian, the matter of priorities is an arrangement of the legitimate. As you learned in the chapter on "The Born-again Life," by the help of God the Christian no longer engages in willfully violating His known will. So now it is a question of how to live out a life that has been surrendered to Him.

There is a biblical plan for priorities that furnishes you with a pattern upon which to build great families and great churches.

Are you willing to take God at His Word? Are you willing to respond quickly to His directions? In Col. 3:1-25 and 4:1, God lays down His priority system.

Conceptually, there are two steps to God's priority system: your relationship to His person and your relationship to His purpose.

I. Your Relationship to His Person

There is little, if any, conflict among those who know Christ as their personal Savior, with regard to their first priority. All Christians agree that nothing is as important as a personal and perpetual relationship with God.

The apostle Paul, in Col. 3:1-10, says:

> Since, then, you have been raised with Christ, set your hearts on things above, where Christ is seated at the right hand of God. Set your minds on things above, not on earthly things. For you died, and your life is now hidden with Christ in God. When Christ, who is your life, appears, then you also will appear with him in glory.
>
> Put to death, therefore, whatever belongs to your earthly nature: sexual immorality, impurity, lust, evil desires and greed, which is idolatry. Because of these, the wrath of God is coming. You used to walk

in these ways, in the life you once lived. But now you must rid yourselves of all such things as these: anger, rage, malice, slander, and
filthy language from your lips. Do not lie to each other, since you have
taken off your old self with its practices and have put on the new self,
which is being renewed in knowledge in the image of its Creator.

This relationship involves the total person. From a functional
point of view, this is what Paul spoke of in 1 Thess. 5:23.

> May your whole spirit, soul and body be kept blameless at the
> coming of our Lord Jesus Christ.

Now the subject of your relationship to His person will be
dealt with as it relates to the threefold functional view of your life,
that is, body, soul, and spirit.

A. Your Physical Life (Body)

> Put to death, therefore, whatever belongs to your earthly nature.
> *(Col. 3:5)*

This verse is saying that if your relationship with God is to be
what it ought to be, you must cease from any physical gratification
that is out of harmony with God's will for you. The word "mortify"
(KJV) ("put to death") means "a turning of the will from self to
God."

B. Your Psychical Life (Soul)

> "In your anger do not sin": Do not let the sun go down while you
> are still angry, and do not give the devil a foothold.   *(Eph. 4:26-27)*

This is a graphic portrayal of the fact that there is an anger that
has its source in the psychical function of the individual and is not
a heart condition. The psychical area includes frustration brought
on by frayed nerves, emotional stress, and fatigue. This is a problem that will always be with us; it must be dealt with properly in
order to maintain the priority of your relationship with God.

There is a difference between an amoral anger of the soul and
the intent to harm another person. Understanding this helps you to
more fully appreciate the way you are made; it also enables you to
ask forgiveness from those you may have offended and to receive
God's forgiveness and cleansing.

By practicing this procedure, you are able to maintain a right
relationship to His person.

C. Your Spiritual Life (Spirit)

> Do not lie to each other, since you have taken off your old self
> with its practices and have put on the new self, which is being re-
> newed in knowledge in the image of its Creator.   *(Col. 3:9-10)*

This passage of Scripture is a graphic portrayal of how priorities encompass the physical, psychical, and spiritual functions in your relationship to His person.

This Colossians passage is a step-by-step explanation of the relationship that you are to establish with God. Until such a relationship with the person of God is created and maintained, it will be impossible to live out this system of biblical priorities. There will be little value in following an arbitrary list of priorities unless a vital relationship to His person is maintained.

II. Your Relationship to His Purpose

Is there anything more exciting than being involved in the purpose of God? The evangelist quotes Jesus as saying that we, His disciples, share the same mission He undertook:

> As thou hast sent me into the world, even so have I also sent them into the world.   *(John 17:18, KJV)*

There are five basic areas in your life: family, church, world, job, and recreation (leisure time). One of the greatest problems is how to prioritize these basic areas. If it were possible to have a static list of priorities to live by, it would not be very exciting or fulfilling.

To graphically portray all of the implications and interplay of your relationship to God's purpose in these five areas would be a needless enterprise. However, there is benefit in discussing the role of each of these areas in relationship to His purpose.

The following diagram will facilitate our discussion:

In this particular illustration, your *job* is taking precedence in time, order, or importance for the moment.

Rather than a static listing of priorities, the model we are espousing is fluid in nature. The priority for any given moment is determined by the interplay between one's perceptual field and how that field is impacted by environmental factors (i.e., family, church, world, job, recreation).

Suppose five different people are involved in a given activity. Although their external behavior may appear somewhat uniform, if you were to ask them what it is that is occupying their primary interest at the moment, the response of each one could well differ from the others. This is the beauty of our humanity. Yet God is able to bring about His purposes through each individual, regardless of the moment-by-moment kaleidoscope of priority arrangements, providing certain criteria are met.

With this kind of individuation, how can we get a handle on developing a system of priorities that applies to every situation? Look again at our diagram and notice that:

● All five of these areas are included in God's purpose for you. Not one of them is outside of His will for you at any time. So we needn't nurse a sense of false guilt due to a specific area assuming momentary priority.

● Each of these areas is tied into your time frame, and the whole pattern is constantly changing.

In the life of the Christian, matters will ascend in priority and occupy our complete attention—yet without producing spiritual conflict so long as we maintain:

● Absolute honesty with God;
● A keen sensitivity to circumstances;
● A willingness to pay whatever price is necessary to fulfill God's purpose;
● Dependence upon the Holy Spirit to reveal the matters that are of the most immediate importance.

The following incidents will illustrate how these principles work in everyday life.

I won't soon forget the morning when the telephone rang and my son said, "Dad, I need to see you as soon as you can arrange it." I turned to my secretary and asked her to rearrange my two appointments at noon and 1 P.M., and said, "Son, I'll see you at noon." As he talked, I was sensitive to the fact that he had moved into the top spot for the moment, and it was pleasing to God that I deal with his need. It was a part of "God's Purpose" for me at that moment.

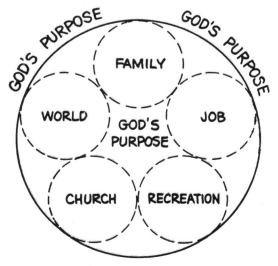

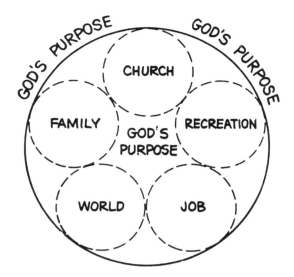

Several days later he called and said, "Dad, I have two good tickets to the pro basketball game, and I want you to go with me." I struggled for a moment because there is no one I would enjoy going with more than him, and no one I'd rather see play my favorite game than the home team. As I thought about my responsibility to the church, the Discipling program, and the people I was to teach, there was an awareness that teaching the class was a part of "God's Purpose" for my life at that moment. I then expressed my sorrow to my son and said, "I'd better teach my class."

One of the enigmas of life is that there are many people who have won their children to their homes and to themselves but have lost them to God and the church. *Can you recall any time when a family has won its children to God and the church but has lost them to its home?*

It is very possible to try to use this *dynamic* priority system as a rationalization to fulfill selfish purposes. However, since all these areas are involved in God's will for you, the only way you could upset God's priority system is to ignore or reject one or more of these four criteria:

- Absolute honesty with God;

- A keen sensitivity to circumstances;

- A willingness to pay whatever price is necessary to fulfill God's purpose;

- Dependence upon the Holy Spirit to reveal His priority system to us as we carry out these functions.

A part of the human dilemma is that we can only be in one place at one time; we can give our attention to only one matter at a time. Choices have to be made. Yet by applying these principles, we can rest in the knowledge that we are discovering God's priorities for our lives.

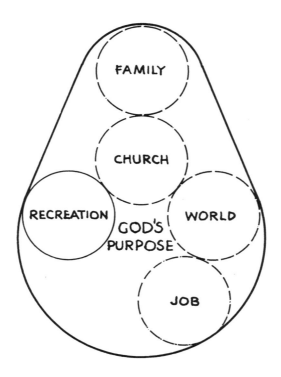

In the previous incident, had the father chosen to go to the ball game with his son rather than teach his Discipling class, this would have been an example of arbitrarily placing his will over God's priority for that moment.

The diagram to the right shows how one personal selfish choice can preempt God's purpose, thereby destroying the harmony of His will.

How many times has God's harmony become discord in your life because you arbitrarily chose your own selfish ambitions over His priorities for you? As an example:

● You may have done this by a failure to be absolutely honest in your relationship to His purpose.

● It may be that you were not as keenly sensitive to the circumstances as you ought to have been. Whatever the cause—moral or amoral—the results may have been the same.

● Perhaps you were not willing to pay the price necessary to carry out God's will.

● Could it have been that your life was so out of balance psychologically or spiritually that you didn't have complete confidence in the fact that the Holy Spirit could and would reveal His desired priority in your life?

Since God's priority system is not a static listing of things, but rather a relationship to His person and purpose, it is important to realize that this system can be thwarted only by the violation of one or more of these principles.

Summary

In this chapter on priorities we have learned that our relationship to God is of primary importance. Based on this right relationship with Him, our relationship with His purpose should naturally follow.

Using a dynamic concept of prioritizing requires that we be in tune with the Holy Spirit. It is easier to miss God's perfect purpose by living according to a static list of priorities than in living by a dynamic concept of prioritizing.

True harmony in the life of today's disciple comes only:

A. When one's relationship to God's person is right;

B. When the five areas (family, church, world, job, recreation) are prioritized in accord with the four criteria:

1. Absolute honesty with God;

2. A keen sensitivity to circumstances;

3. A willingness to pay whatever price necessary to fulfill God's purpose;

4. Dependence upon the Holy Spirit to reveal His priority system to us as we carry out these functions.

Living a life of faith, increasingly learning the art of prayer, knowing God's will, being committed fully to Him, following in obedience, living by biblical priorities—all of these factors are building blocks that will help us face temptation successfully. Chapter 12 will give us an opportunity to study temptation more thoroughly.

12

Temptation

Introduction

Summary

In Him we have peace. In Him we have power!
Preserved by His grace throughout the dark hour.
In all our temptations He keeps us, to prove
His utmost salvation, His fulness of love.

—*John Wesley*

12

Temptation

Throughout this study you will learn that God is glorified when we worship Him by making right choices. In previous chapters we have alluded to the fact that we are continually confronted with alternatives of right and wrong. True Christian character is partially established by making right choices. Your response to temptation will reveal the true object of your faith. Jesus tells us plainly that He is to be the Object of our faith: "If you love *Me,* you will obey *Me;* and if you obey *Me, I* will reveal myself to you" (see John 14:21, TLB). Therefore, temptation is not to be taken lightly, for within each occasion of temptation there is the opportunity for either "growth in grace" or "growth in grief."

For the purpose of this study, *temptation* is defined as
> an endeavor to persuade a person to select a specific alternative by means of argument and influence. (This usually, but not always, carries with it the idea of being tempted to do evil.)

The two words listed below convey meanings that are integral to our understanding of temptation. Let's take a moment to become reacquainted with them:

- *Confrontation*
  Simply being presented with at least two alternatives.

- *Conflict*
  This is the battle for moral mastery of the heart. When the born-again Christian becomes aware that there are two spirits (the sinful spirit and the Holy Spirit) within, then this contention begins to take shape.

It is important that you draw a clear distinction here between *conflict* in a theological sense (old nature against new nature) as opposed to *conflict* in the general sense (pain, disease, weather).

Temptation need not be something to fear. It need not be a threat at all. In fact, this chapter contains three liberating truths about temptation.

I. Temptation is natural. Natural in the sense that all of us are confronted with it regularly.

II. Temptation is neutral. Neutral in the sense that in and of itself it is not sinful.

III. Temptation is necessary. Necessary in that all of humankind is in its probation period, choosing to obey or disobey while here on earth.

I. Temptation Is Natural

> No temptation has seized you except what is common to man. And God is faithful; he will not let you be tempted beyond what you can bear. But when you are tempted, he will also provide a way out so that you can stand up under it.
> *(1 Cor. 10:13)*

The confusion that exists among Christians with regard to temptation is staggering. There are two prominent areas of confusion that you need to consider:

• Some reason with themselves: "If a person is filled with the Holy Spirit, how can it be possible to feel or react in a way that is out of harmony with God's perfect will?"

• Others—perhaps the majority among Christians—reason: "If I am hounded by evil thoughts or am desiring evil ways, yet I know I am a Christian, then the only conclusion to reach is that I am compelled to sin 'in thought, word, and deed' every day."

You see, they identify "evil thoughts" as sin. They have not fully understood that thoughts of evil are natural, not sinful.

Temptation is experienced through the natural functions of the body, soul, and spirit. God is glorified as we freely choose righteousness through the exercise of body, soul, and spirit. God allowed humankind to be subjected to temptation, knowing full well they would fall. God gave humankind full rein to make choices, for in the capacity to choose lies the capacity to love. Without this capacity we would be reduced to an automaton—a mere mechanical robot. As it is, our capacities to choose are motivated by the quest of our natural desires for personal gain. Dr. W. T. Purkiser said, "Man is tempted to use his natural desires in a wrong way or for a wrong goal. Unless there is desire, there is no temptation."[1]

With the possible exception of those who suffer certain physical or psychological impairments, we all share the same natural susceptibilities to sin. Our greatest area of vulnerability is our personal set of likes, dislikes, and needs. For instance, if we had no interest or love for sports, we would experience little or no temptation to desecrate the Sabbath by going to a ball game instead of to church.

To help you identify your own vulnerabilities, list the areas in your life in which you are most susceptible to temptation.

1. _____

2. _____

3. _____

---

1. Purkiser, *Exploring Our Christian Faith*, 430.

II. Temptation Is Neutral

> For we do not have a high priest who is unable to sympathize with our weaknesses, but we have one who has been tempted in every way, just as we are—yet was without sin.   *(Heb. 4:15)*

Down through the years many good, sincere Christians have been robbed of living a victorious life because they did not understand the fact that temptation is neutral. They were taught that even the slightest evil thought passing through their conscious mind was absolute proof that they were still evil. How sad; that kind of teaching brings about insurmountable confusion. People so taught often fall out of the fear of falling.

But God's Word clearly teaches that temptation becomes sin only when, in your heart, you yield to that temptation and choose to disobey God. James makes this clear in chapter 1:

> But each one is tempted when he is carried away and enticed by his own lust. Then when lust has conceived, it gives birth to sin; and when sin is accomplished, it brings forth death.   *(vv. 14-15, NASB)*

James is saying here that when your natural desires are conceived (that is, responded to by your will), then this gives birth to sin. To say it another way: When you use your natural desires in a way that is contrary to the Scriptures, you have sinned.

Here are two illustrations:

● There is nothing wrong with the desire to eat. But to steal the food to satisfy the need to eat is sin.

● There is nothing wrong with the desire for sex. But to have sexual relations outside the sanctity of marriage is sin.

Discovering the difference between temptation and sin has brought liberation to many Christians. Remember: Temptation never results in sin until you, in your heart, say yes to something contrary to God's will.

Keeping in mind this definition of *temptation*, fill in the box:

```
1. Define the act of sin: _____

_____

_____

2. State what sin brings: _____

_____

_____
```

In conclusion, reflect on the statement of Dr. L. T. Corlett:

> Temptation is always accompanied by a desire to follow the sug-

gestion. First in the process the attention is drawn either to a mental contemplation or to an object outside of man. If that attention is centered on either one, a legitimate desire is aroused for that object. The suggestion is made from the tempter that it would be advantageous to enjoy the situation. The next step is the suggestion of how to obtain this end. Then the will is attached and the individual must make a decision as to whether or not the suggestion for satisfaction in an illegitimate manner will be carried out.

The desire will at times be very strong and it may last for a period of time, but the guilt and condemnation do not come to an individual because of the desire. Temptation has not become sin simply because desire has been awakened. *Temptation becomes sin only when the will decides in favor of the suggestion of the tempter.* At times the battle is intense . . . but, as long as the will is held steady in alignment with the will of God and against the suggestion to evil, the individual has not sinned.[2]

III. Temptation Is Necessary

James makes clear the reason we experience temptation in this probation period of life:

> Consider it pure joy, my brothers, whenever you face trials of many kinds, because you know that the testing of your faith develops perseverance. Perseverance must finish its work so that you may be mature and complete, not lacking anything.   *(1:2-4)*

Sensitive Christians want their character to reflect the Spirit of Christ. One of the ways this happens is through meeting and mastering temptation. Choosing alternatives that are consistent with God's Word insures the development of Christlikeness within us.

Though the heart is *affected* by the natural amoral desires and needs of man, it is *controlled* ultimately by either the sinful nature or the spiritual nature within it.

Paul explains this twofold issue in Romans chapters 7 and 8.

● In Rom. 7:22-25, he describes the person who is wrestling with the desire to honor God, but yet experiences the presence of original sin.

> For in my inner being I delight in God's law; but I see another law at work in the members of my body, waging war against the law of my mind and making me a prisoner of the law of sin at work within my members. What a wretched man I am! Who will rescue me from this body of death? Thanks be to God—through Jesus Christ our Lord!

● In Rom. 8:1-4, he explains the weakness of the law and the sinful nature and assures us that when we are set free from this sinful nature by the power of the Holy Spirit, we can be victorious over temptation.

---

2. Lewis T. Corlett, *Holiness in Practical Living* (Kansas City: Beacon Hill Press, 1948), 56.

Therefore, there is now no condemnation for those who are in Christ Jesus, because through Christ Jesus the law of the Spirit of life set me free from the law of sin and death. For what the law was powerless to do in that it was weakened by the sinful nature, God did by sending his own Son in the likeness of sinful man to be a sin offering. And so he condemned sin in sinful man, in order that the righteous requirements of the law might be fully met in us, who do not live according to the sinful nature but according to the Spirit.

God knows that if you defeat the enemy of your life through the power of His Spirit, you will become more like Him in all that you do. So instead of temptations being stumbling blocks, they are potentially stepping-stones to helping us become like Christ.

This is enough to make you want to rejoice with John as he said, "Greater is He who is in you than he who is in the world" (1 John 4:4, NASB)!

Temptation need not be a source of worry for us if we keep clearly in mind these truths:

- Temptation is natural, in that it comes through the natural, human desires and functions of man.

- Temptation is neutral, in that temptation, in and of itself, is neither righteous nor evil.

- Temptation is necessary in this probation period of life, to develop character.

Jesus had to experience the same set of temptations that each of us does. He knows what it is to feel the pressure of natural desires upon His psyche.

> For we do not have a high priest who is unable to sympathize with our weaknesses, but we have one who has been tempted in every way, just as we are—yet was without sin.
> Let us then approach the throne of grace with confidence, so that we may receive mercy and find grace to help us in our time of need.
>
> *(Heb. 4:15-16)*

Matt. 4:1-11 records three areas in which temptation was experienced in the life of Jesus.

A. Physically

> Then Jesus was led by the Spirit into the desert to be tempted by the devil. After fasting forty days and forty nights, he was hungry. The tempter came to him and said, "If you are the Son of God, tell these stones to become bread."
> Jesus answered, "It is written: 'Man does not live on bread alone, but on every word that comes from the mouth of God.'" *(Matt. 4:1-4)*

This passage describes Satan's initial efforts to tempt Jesus. It is frequently his pattern to appeal first to our physical needs.

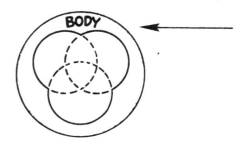

> The tempter . . . said, "If you are the Son of God, tell these stones to become bread."

Satan commonly solicits the physical desires of the Christian, using cars, houses, clothes, food, sex, and other material things as bait.

B. Psychically

> Then the devil took him to the holy city and had him stand on the highest point of the temple. "If you are the Son of God," he said, "throw yourself down. For it is written:
> 'He will command his angels concerning you, and they will lift you up in their hands, so that you will not strike your foot against a stone.'"
> Jesus answered him, "It is also written: 'Do not put the Lord your God to the test.'"   *(Matt. 4:5-7)*

Satan, in his subtle way, appealed to Jesus' psychical needs. Being human, Jesus had the same psychical needs that every human being has.

How often people are tempted to try the spectacular, to do the extraordinary thing to gain acceptance. They are also tempted to dominate or intimidate others.

> "If you are the Son of God . . . throw yourself down. For it is written: 'He will command his angels concerning you.'"

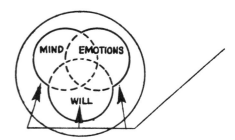

C. Spiritually

> Again, the devil took him to a very high mountain and showed him all the kingdoms of the world and their splendor. "All this I will give you," he said, "if you will bow down and worship me."
> Jesus said to him, "Away from me, Satan! For it is written: 'Worship the Lord your God, and serve him only.'"
> Then the devil left him, and angels came and attended him.
>   *(Matt. 4:8-11)*

Failing to get Jesus to yield physically and psychically, Satan moved to the most crucial area of His being—His spirit.

This is the control center; this is the most critical function in life. This is where the decision is made to become a slave either to the spirit of Satan or to the Spirit of God.

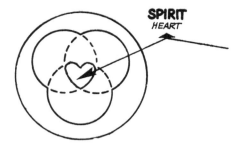

"All this I will give you," he said, "if you will bow down and worship me."

Even the most mature Christian is vulnerable to this enticement to misguided worship. Humankind is incurably religious. Veiled worship that is self-centered or self-indulgent often goes unrecognized for what it is.

Jesus never answered Satan with a simple "No." He answered him with the only offensive weapon the Christian has—the Word of God. In Eph. 6:17 Paul calls this weapon "the sword of the Spirit, which is the word of God."

James describes the reward of those who face temptations victoriously:

> Blessed is the man who perseveres under trial, because when he has stood the test, he will receive the crown of life that God has promised to those who love him.   *(1:12)*

Stop and list the areas of your life where you are most susceptible to yielding sinfully to a natural desire:

1. _____
2. _____
3. _____
4. _____

Our adversary is shrewd and persistent. He crafts every temptation to meet your mood.

John Wesley assessed Satan's strategies well:

> As the most dangerous winds may enter at little openings, so the devil never enters more dangerously than by little unobserved incidents, which seem to be nothing, yet insensibly open the heart to great temptations.[3]

Being greatly tempted does not have to preclude victory. Jesus

---

3. Wesley, "Plain Account," 439.

has broken the way through temptation that opens to the Father. "Greater is he that is in you, than he that is in the world" (1 John 4:4, KJV).

Summary

Throughout history temptation has been a great source of worry for the Christian. But temptation need not be a source of worry for us if we understand that:

1. Temptation is natural in that it comes through our natural desires and functions;

2. Temptation is neutral in that it is neither righteous nor evil;

3. Temptation is necessary in this probation period of life—it is the means by which character is developed within us.

Jesus is our Pattern for how to handle temptation successfully. He knows what it is to feel the *full impact* of the pressure of temptation.

> For we do not have a high priest who is unable to sympathize with our weaknesses, but we have one who has been tempted in every way, just as we are—yet was without sin.   *(Heb. 4:15)*

Matt. 4:1-11 records how Jesus was tempted to give in to His physical desires, how He was tempted to choose Satan's plan in order to satisfy a psychical need, and how Satan even tried to get Jesus to worship him and thus sidestep the mission for which He was sent. In each case Jesus answered Satan with the Sword of the Spirit, the Word of God. This is the pattern each of us must follow in order to successfully handle our adversary, remembering that the Victor is on our side!

> Let us then approach the throne of grace with confidence, so that we may receive mercy and find grace to help us in our time of need.
> *(Heb. 4:16).*

An area in which Satan wants to defeat us more than in any other is witnessing. He would use every weapon at his disposal to tempt us to not witness. This is a particularly keen issue with Satan, for, if he can prevent God's people from witnessing, he can short-circuit God's purpose in sending His Holy Spirit.

God's Word describes how Satan shall be defeated by the saints: "They defeated him by the *blood of the Lamb,* and by their *testimony*" (Rev. 12:11, TLB, italics added). Chapter 13 teaches us how to fulfill the Great Commission through personal evangelism.

13

Personal Evangelism

Give me one hundred preachers who fear nothing but sin and desire nothing but God, and I care not a straw whether they be clergymen or laymen; such alone will shake the gates of hell and set up the "kingdom of heaven on earth."

—*John Wesley*

13

Personal Evangelism

Evangelism: A preaching of, or a zealous effort to
   spread, the gospel.—*Webster*

In the previous 12 chapters of this material, you have been presented with the basic concepts that will help you not only enter into a vital relationship with Christ but also become an established, victorious Christian. However, there is now an additional step that you must take. The Master wants you to be not only a *disciple* but also a *discipler.* There is no way you can fulfill the Great Commission without *sharing* your faith. The sharing of this great new life with those around you will be accomplished through *personal evangelism.*

Perhaps the most encouraging single revelation in the evangelical world today is the vast army of unused laypersons! This is the *most strategic key* to evangelizing the world. You are a part of that great potential army. Only when you become *trained, motivated,* and *involved* will you be able to *change your world.* What if this sleeping army would awaken and confront the known world with the claims of the gospel? What a privilege it is to be a part of that awakening army through personal evangelism!

The subject of personal evangelism will be presented in this chapter and will include the following areas for your consideration:

   I. The Principles of Personal Evangelism
   II. The Problems of Personal Evangelism
   III. The Pedagogy of Personal Evangelism
   IV. The Presentation of Personal Evangelism

I. The Principles of Personal Evangelism

A. Every Christian Must Be a Witness

Christ's directive to "go and make disciples" (Matt. 28:19) does not make allowance for any exceptions. There is no logic flexible enough to release any Christian from this order. Exactly how and when you are to witness is not clearly revealed. But the *necessity of your witnessing is essential.*

Christ began His ministry with the words, "Come, follow me, . . . and I will make you fishers of men" (Matt. 4:19). *He closed His ministry* with the words "Go and make disciples" (28:19). The discipling activities of the Early Church are recorded in the Book of Acts. The first-century Church was characterized *by its love and enthusiasm for personal evangelism.*

B. Every Christian Must Be a Trainee

There is no way you can become proficient in any area without training.

> Study to shew thyself approved unto God, a workman that needeth not to be ashamed, rightly dividing the word of truth.
>
> *(2 Tim. 2:15, KJV)*

The imperative declared here by Paul is not for the clergy alone—it is for everyone! More than 99 percent of the Christian world is composed of laypersons. If this great, potential army of laypeople is to be *effective, it must be trained.* The duty of the Christian minister is to see to the training of believers.

> It was he who gave some to be apostles, some to be prophets, some to be evangelists, and some to be pastors and teachers, to prepare God's people for works of service, so that the body of Christ may be built up.   *(Eph. 4:11-12)*

As a disciple, you must be involved in a program of becoming better equipped to share your faith.

C. Every Christian Must Be a Trainer

Professional ministers are not the only ones who need to be trained. Neither are these ministers the only ones who need to be *actively involved in training others.* There is a limit to the number of people any professional minister or church leader can train.

Some years ago in industry, there was a study undertaken to determine the number of people any one person could supervise effectively. The results of that study show that, in most cases, one person could effectively supervise only 7 to 12 people.

Dr. James Kennedy has claimed that 95 percent of those who are Christians never lead anyone else to Christ. Part of the problem lies in the lack of sufficient numbers of trainers. You, and all of the born-again believers that you know, must become actively involved in training others if the masses of the world are to be confronted with the claims of the gospel.

II. The Problems of Personal Evangelism

It won't take you long, if you honestly want to share your faith with those in your world, to learn that there are problems inherent in this great task of evangelism. The mistaken idea is that, because you are dealing with spiritual issues, God will automatically remove all obstacles. This is unrealistic. You cannot ignore problems and simply expect them to go away. This is not only foolish but also fatal. Perhaps the three most pressing problems are:

- Fear of Failure
- Facing Objections
- Finding New Prospects

A. Fear of Failure

Essentially, the problem of fear arises from three sources:

- A sense of inadequacy
- An overactive imagination
- Uncertainty of the other person's intention

1. *A sense of inadequacy*

A sense of inadequacy may stem from an:

- Inadequate understanding
- Inadequate spiritual experience
- Inadequate communication training

a. If you sense a fear of inadequacy, stemming from what appears to be a lack of understanding, go back and review chapters 3 ("The Human Experience"), 4 ("The Born-again Life"), and 5 ("The Spirit-filled Life"). It is further suggested that you pray, asking God for wisdom.

James, in his Epistle, states,

> If any of you lacks wisdom, he should ask God, who gives generously to all without finding fault, and it will be given to him.   *(1:5)*

b. If your fear comes from an inadequate relationship with Christ, it must be immediately remedied. A present, vital relationship with Christ is an imperative. The point of greatest encouragement is that God wants continuous fellowship with you. His drawing, and your responding, will reestablish that fellowship.

c. If your fear is based on a feeling of inadequate communication training, you are now reading the appropriate chapter. This chapter will explore the techniques of approach, presentation, and follow-up. When you complete this chapter, you will have some practical handles for presenting the claims of the gospel.

2. *An overactive imagination*

Many times an overactive imagination creates situations and

conjures up pictures that do not exist—and probably never will. A subtle fear is to presume that, because of a person's position or abilities, that one does not need God. This is a trick of Satan to defeat you and the person to whom God has led you. The personal evangelist must remember that *everyone needs what Christ has to offer.*

3. *Uncertainty of the other person's intention*

Another cause of fear is the uncertainty of the prospect's intentions, possible reactions, and ultimate response. The command of Jesus was simple: "Go and tell." The responsibility for the results of that sharing does not lie with the personal evangelist—*but with the Holy Spirit.* Your success is judged, not on whether the person to whom you witness accepts Christ, but rather on the fact *that you have shared.* This should eliminate the fear of failure for those who share.

> But if you warn him to repent and he doesn't, he will die in his sin, and you will not be responsible. *(Ezek. 33:9, TLB)*

B. Facing Objections

When you present the gospel, you can expect to face some objections. This is because you are dealing with pride, prejudice, preconceived ideas, and the influence of a personal devil. *The way you face these objections* may tend to be influenced by your own personality.

Some will meet the objections head-on. *Some will* push the "panic button." *Others will* "shrink," "fall back," and even "freeze."

However, you must accept these objections with grace. You are to be more interested in winning *a person* than winning *a point.* When someone questions your statement, or specifically disagrees with you, the best way to keep the issue *objective,* and not *subjective,* is to say, "Thank you for that point; I really appreciate it." As a result the person is kept from being on the defensive.

Are you really looking for objections? The answer is "No!" But it is always good when the person with whom you are dealing feels free to object and feels as though you are willing to face any question he or she might have.

Here are three ways you can face objections:

- The objection may be simple and may not hinder your presentation. If so, deal with it *simply* and *quickly.*

- If it is something you will be dealing with later in your presentation, simply state, "That is a good point; and we will talk about it in a few minutes if this is all right."

- There is a possibility that some questions or objections will be presented to you that you are unable to answer. First of all, don't be embarrassed or threatened. Just simply take out a pen or pencil, write them down, and tell the person that you are going to find the answers. This kind of interest, and careful writing of the questions, shows genuineness and concern.

C. Finding New Prospects

There has never been a day in modern history when prospects seemed more available than today. The *awareness of need*, the popularity and *acceptance of evangelical Christianity*, the *futility of affluence* and artificiality, and the *belief in Christ's soon return* all tend to make people willing to discuss spiritual matters.

In the church, there are several ways that have proved helpful in contacting new prospects.

1. *People visiting your own local church* are some of the best prospects. This is because:

a. they have visited with those of you who will be coming to visit them;

b. they have received help from your service that they attended;

c. they have felt the warmth of the Body of Christ, which helps to break down prejudices and preconceived ideas.

2. *Parents of the Sunday School children* in your church are also *prime prospects.* This is because:

a. they normally appreciate your interest in their families;

b. they should feel guilt for not being to their children what they ought to be spiritually;

c. they probably have a deep, though not always acknowledged, desire to have a right relationship with God.

3. *People in your own surroundings* can be some of the *most likely prospects.* New people in your community and community service groups are only a few of the potentials for prospects.

Whatever system is used, there must be a constant realization that there are more prospects than there are converts. This means that you and your church must be constantly reaching out to a hurting world if you are to carry out the Great Commission.

> A man's worst enemies will be right in his own home! If you love your father and mother more than you love me, you are not worthy of being mine; or if you love your son or daughter more than me, you are not worthy of being mine. If you refuse to take up your cross and follow me, you are not worthy of being mine." *(Matt. 10:36-38, TLB)*

III. The Pedagogy of Personal Evangelism

As you will recall from chapter 1, "Mandate of the Master," the basic teaching method of this entire Discipling Curriculum has been:

- Understand
- Experience
- Communicate

In chapters 3, 4, and 5—"The Human Experience," "The Born-again Life," and "The Spirit-filled Life"—the major emphasis was on *understanding* and *experiencing.* Chapters 6—12 centered around the *concepts of spiritual growth* through *understanding* and *experiencing.* In this chapter on "Personal Evangelism," you will apply the third ingredient of *communicating* those things that you have understood and experienced. It is important now for you to apply this same pedagogy (understand, experience, communicate) to personal evangelism.

A. Understand

There are many Christians within the fellowship of the church who possess a spiritual experience that *far surpasses their understanding.* This need not—and should not—be true. If you are going to be an effective personal evangelist, you will need to *know what it means to be* human (chapter 3, "The Human Experience") and *our condition* prior to conversion (chapter 4, "The Born-again Life").

The degree to which you understand *human spiritual need* and *God's provision* will have a direct bearing on your effectiveness.

B. Experience

There are some within the church, and many outside it, who have an *understanding of spiritual issues far beyond their experience.* There are few instances when you, as a personal evangelist, will lead someone else to an experience with Christ beyond what you presently possess.

Perhaps the greatest single factor going for you as a personal evangelist is *your own personal relationship with God.* There are three elements that contribute to your experience:

- your spiritual condition
- your consistency
- your credibility

Your good life will do much to prepare the heart of the possible convert.

When a personal evangelist is sensitive to the Spirit of God, the timing, wording, and atmosphere of personal witness all work together.

C. Communicate

Once understanding and experience are in harmony, you are in a position to share Jesus Christ. The word *communicate* has its basis in the word *commune*, which simply means "to share" or "to have in common." It could best be expressed in terms of the personal evangelist as "one person sharing with another the message of salvation."

Perhaps the greatest single reason for a formal study of personal evangelism is to prepare you to the very greatest degree possible to help you communicate what you have learned and experienced during these first 12 chapters.

IV. The Presentation of Personal Evangelism

As a review, please list the eight elements included in the Born-again Crisis.

BORN-AGAIN CRISIS

```
                    List the Four Responses
    1. _____
    2. _____
    3. _____
    4. _____
```

```
                    List the Four Results
    1. _____
    2. _____
    3. _____
    4. _____
```

Also, list the eight elements included in the Spirit-filled Crisis.

SPIRIT-FILLED CRISIS

```
                    List the Four Responses
    1. _____
    2. _____
    3. _____
    4. _____
```

Notes

List the Four Results
1. _____
2. _____
3. _____
4. _____

It is the intention of this chapter to *equip* you with some *simple, practical handles* that will enable you to *share* that which you have learned in the previous chapters. You are now going to be able to *share this Good News with those around you.*

Recall the diagram describing the Discipling Building Blocks. Notice how the fulfillment of the "Mandate of the Master" is achieved through the final step of "Personal Evangelism." This process becomes the *life cycle of the true disciple.*

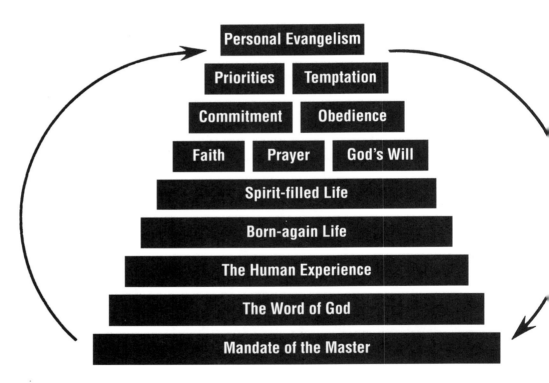

The Discipling Building Blocks are designed to bring you from the point of being a *disciple* to that of becoming a *discipler*. This section of the chapter on "Personal Evangelism" will be divided into three sections:

- Basic Outline
- Outline plus Reasons and Scriptures
- Sample Presentation in Conversation Form

A. Basic Outline

1. *Qualification:* To identify the position of the prospect
    a. *Approach No. 1*—To prospects who have attended your church
        (1) Identify their secular background
        (2) Identify their church background
        (3) Identify their relationship with your church
        (4) Identify their relationship with God

    > Go to either the Presentation for the Born-again Life (2) or the Presentation for the Spirit-filled Life (4).

    b. *Approach No. 2*—To prospects who have not attended your church
        (1) Identify their secular background
        (2) Identify their church background
        (3) Identify their relationship with God

    > Go to either the Presentation for the Born-again Life (2) or the Presentation for the Spirit-filled Life (4).

2. *Presentation for the Born-again Life*
    a. Divine Initiative
    b. Awareness of Need
    c. Awareness of Moral Choice
    d. Our Response

3. *Follow-through and Discipleship After Presentation and Acceptance of the Born-again Life*
    a. Forgiveness
    b. Justification
    c. Regeneration
    d. Adoption
    e. Involvement

4. *Presentation for the Spirit-filled Life*
    a. Divine Initiative
    b. Awareness of Need
    c. Awareness of Moral Choice
    d. Our Response

5. *Follow-through and Discipleship After Presentation and Acceptance of the Spirit-filled Life*
    a. Heart Purity
    b. Heart Perfection
    c. Infilling of the Holy Spirit
    d. Empowering of the Holy Spirit
    e. Involvement

B. Outline plus Reasons and Scriptures

1. Qualification

It is important to qualify prospects by identifying their position regarding both secular and spiritual life. If you are going to help meet a person's need, you must *first identify the need*. The approach will be varied based upon whether the prospect's acquaintance was made through the church or the workaday world.

> a. *Approach No. 1—To prospects who have attended your church*
> > (1) *Identify their secular background*
> > *Reason:* to establish rapport and find a common ground for communication.
> > (2) *Identify their church background*
> > *Reason:* to establish rapport, to discover the prospects' past theological affiliation, and to determine the attitude they maintain toward their church and background.
> > (3) *Identify their relationship with your church*
> > *Reason:* to establish rapport by allowing them to disclose their feelings and responses to *your church* and its ministry.
> > (4) *Identify their relationship with God*
> > *Reason:* based upon, and utilizing, the rapport that has been established, *determine their present spiritual position* and *discover their need*. The *outcome* of this identification *will determine* whether this visit should become a *situation for the presentation of the gospel*, or simply a *public relations visit*, in which you proceed to find out how your church can serve them.
>
> b. *Approach No. 2—To prospects who have not attended your church* (same as Approach No. 1—except "Identify their relationship with your church" has been left out)
> > (1) Identify their secular background
> > (2) Identify their church background
> > (3) Identify their relationship with God

2. Presentation for the Born-again Life

> a. *Divine Initiative*—God reaching out to all
>
> > *For God so loved* the world that *he gave* his one and only Son, that whoever believes in him shall not perish but have eternal life.
> > *(John 3:16, italics added)*
>
> > But God commendeth his love toward us, in that, *while we were yet sinners*, Christ died for us.   *(Rom. 5:8, KJV, italics added)*
>
> b. *Awareness of Need*—Recognition of our sinful condition
>
> > For *all have sinned* and fall short of the glory of God.
> > *(Rom. 3:23, italics added)*
>
> > And He, when *He* comes, *will convict* the world concerning sin, and righteousness, and judgment.   *(John 16:8, NASB, italics added)*

c. *Awareness of Moral Choice*—Awareness of realizing moral responsibility

> *Whoever believes [puts his faith] in the Son* has eternal life, but *whoever rejects the Son* will not see [that] life, for God's wrath remains on him. *(John 3:36, italics added)*

d. *Our Response*—Responding to moral responsibility

> Here I am! I stand at the door and knock. *If anyone hears* my voice *and opens* the door, I will come in and eat with him, and he with me. *(Rev. 3:20, italics added)*

> *If we confess* our sins, *he is faithful* and just and will forgive us our sins and purify us from all unrighteousness. *(1 John 1:9, italics added)*

3. Follow-through and Discipleship After Presentation and Acceptance of the Born-again Life

This section is to be used to explain to the new disciple *what has happened in his life.*

a. *Forgiveness*—the pardon is given to free us from the penalty of our sinful acts

> All the prophets testify about him that everyone who believes in him receives *forgiveness* of sins through his name.
> *(Acts 10:43, italics added)*

> If we confess our sins, he is faithful and just and *will forgive us* our sins and purify us from all unrighteousness. *(1 John 1:9, italics added)*

b. *Justification*—*just as if* you had never sinned; a legal act of satisfying the Law

> God presented him as a sacrifice of atonement, through faith in his blood. He did this to demonstrate his *justice.*
> *(Rom. 3:25, italics added)*

c. *Regeneration*—to be "born again"; new life through Christ

> Therefore, if anyone is in Christ, he is a *new creation;* the old has gone, the *new has come!* *(2 Cor. 5:17, italics added)*

d. *Adoption*—being received into the family of God with all privileges of sonship

> So you are no longer a slave, *but a son;* and since you are a son, God has made you *also an heir.* *(Gal. 4:7, italics added)*

> The Spirit himself testifies with our spirit that we are *God's children.* Now if *we are children,* then *we are heirs*—heirs of God and *co-heirs with Christ.* *(Rom. 8:16-17, italics added)*

e. *Involvement*

After a prospect has become a born-again Christian, help him or her to get *involved* immediately in an *active discipling group.* This gives opportunity to become exposed to the "Mandate of the Master," to experience God's plan and design for *growth,* and to learn how to share one's personal witness through *personal evangelism.*

4. Presentation for the Spirit-filled Life

NOTE: Use this presentation only after the qualifying of the prospect has determined the need for the Spirit-filled life.

Diagram the twofold aspect of sin.

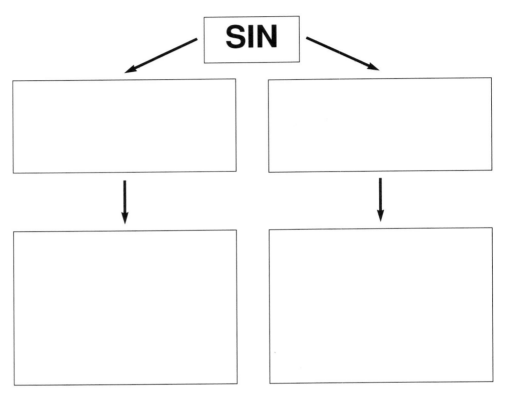

a. *Divine Initiative*—God reaching out to deliver us from indwelling sin

> And so Jesus also suffered outside the city gate to make the *people holy* through his own blood.   *(Heb. 13:12, italics added)*

b. *Awareness of Need*—Recognizing our sinful nature

> What a wretched man I am! Who will rescue me from this body of death?   *(Rom. 7:24)*

> Blessed are they which do hunger and thirst after righteousness: for they shall be filled.   *(Matt. 5:6, KJV)*

c. *Awareness of Moral Choice*—Realizing one's responsibility to seek deliverance from indwelling sin

> But just as he who called you is holy, so be holy in all you do; for it is written: *"Be holy, because I am holy."*   *(1 Pet. 1:15-16, italics added)*

d. *Our Response*—Reacting to one's need for the Spirit-filled life

> *Present your bodies a living sacrifice*, holy, acceptable unto God, which is your reasonable service.   *(Rom. 12:1, KJV, italics added)*

5. Follow-through and Discipleship After Presentation and Acceptance of the Spirit-filled Life

This section is to be used to explain to the new Spirit-filled disciple *what has happened.*

a. *Heart Purity*—God's act of cleaning your heart from the pollution of original sin

> He made no distinction between us and them, for he *purified their hearts by faith.* (Acts 15:9, italics added)

> Cleanse your hands, ye sinners; and *purify your hearts, ye double minded.* (James 4:8, KJV, italics added)

b. *Heart Perfection*—restoration of God's moral nature through perfected affections and motives

> May God himself, the God of peace, *sanctify you through and through.* (1 Thess. 5:23, italics added)

> *Be perfect,* therefore, *as your heavenly Father* is perfect. (Matt. 5:48, italics added)

> Herein is *our love made perfect,* that we may have boldness in the day of judgment: because as he is, *so are we in this world.* (1 John 4:17, KJV, italics added)

c. *Infilling of the Holy Spirit*—the Holy Spirit fills and abides within the heart of the believer

> *Be filled* with the Spirit. (Eph. 5:18, italics added)

> And he shall give you another Comforter, that he may *abide with you* for ever . . . for *he dwelleth with you,* and *shall be in you.* (John 14:16-17, KJV, italics added)

d. *Empowering of the Holy Spirit*—the power that is received when the Holy Spirit comes to abide

> "But you will *receive power* when the Holy Spirit comes on you." (Acts 1:8, italics added)

> But tarry ye in the city of Jerusalem, until ye be endued with power from on high. (Luke 24:49, KJV)

e. *Involvement*

After a prospect has received the Holy Spirit, help him or her to get involved immediately in an active discipling group. This will give opportunity to become exposed to the "Mandate of the Master," to experience God's plan and design for *growth,* and to learn how to share one's personal witness of being *born-again* and *Spirit-filled* through *personal evangelism.*

C. Sample Presentation in Conversation Form

We live in a world where the artificial and insincere seem to dominate interpersonal relationships. If a person says, "I really care about you," the question may arise in your mind, "What do they really want?" or "What strings are attached?"

Everyone seeks genuineness in personal relationships. We are looking for *that one person who is sincerely and genuinely interested in us*—a person in whom we can place our trust. To become a person in whom trust is placed, you must *earn the right* by being sincerely interested in the other person. You must establish identification with that person in order for you to share Christ.

> When I am with those whose consciences bother them easily, *I don't act as though I know it all* and don't say they are foolish; the result is that they are willing to let me help them. Yes, whatever a person is like, *I try to find common ground with him so that he will let me tell him about Christ* and let Christ save him. *I do this to get the Gospel to them* and also for the blessing I myself receive when I see them come to Christ. *(1 Cor. 9:22-23, TLB, italics added)*

1. Qualification: To Identify the Position of the Prospect
(Memorize all Key Statements, Key Questions, and Key Scriptures.)

a. Approach No. 1—To prospects who have attended your church

(1) *Identify their secular background*

Those first few moments of introduction and conversation are very important. To be overly serious would be disastrous. Occasionally, a bit of humor and light conversation will help you open the door to friendship with them.

KEY STATEMENT	Example: "HELLO, MR. AND MRS. BROWN, MY NAME IS CHARLIE SMITH, AND I'M FROM _____ CHURCH. WE WERE DELIGHTED TO HAVE YOU AND YOUR FAMILY WORSHIP WITH US A FEW DAYS AGO. WE WANTED TO COME BY AND VISIT WITH YOU FOR A LITTLE WHILE."

As you enter the house and are ready to be seated, be aware of something about which to converse, such as trophies, musical instruments, family portraits, plants, antiques, and so on. Be sure you are talking about *their interests, their lives, their families,* and the *non-controversial* matters of interest to them. Do *not* talk about yourself or your interests *except as they relate to them,* and then only briefly.

(2) *Identify their church background*

If you can become aware, to some degree, of their theological background, their depth of training, and special interests, you will be better prepared to handle the questions that may arise.

KEY STATEMENT	"WHAT AN EXCITING DAY TO BE A PART OF A GOOD CHURCH!"

KEY QUESTION	"WHAT CHURCH DO YOU REGULARLY ATTEND?"

(3) *Identify their relationship with your church*

KEY QUESTION	"HOW DID YOU HAPPEN TO VISIT OUR CHURCH?"

If their answer is friends, special services, or advertising, you may wish to respond, *"That's exciting, Mr. Brown. We are always interested in the way people learn about our church!"* If friends, *"They're such nice folk"* (if you know them). If special services, *"That was an especially meaningful time for me."* If advertising, *"That was an attractive ad or commercial."*

<table>
<tr><td>**KEY QUESTION**</td><td>"WHAT DID YOU LIKE BEST ABOUT OUR CHURCH?"</td></tr>
</table>

(a) If they speak to a particular ministry, such as the music or the pastor's message, your response may be: *"More than anything else, we want to be a church that sincerely cares about meeting the needs of people in our world. Every ministry in our church is committed to this end."*

(b) If they speak about the warmth and friendliness of the congregation, your response may be: *"The reason that you sensed that warmth and friendliness is because our relationship to Christ is the most meaningful experience in our lives."* *Note:* Regardless of their response, continue with this KEY STATEMENT in a *reflective manner.*

<table>
<tr><td>**KEY STATEMENT**</td><td>"AS I LOOK BACK OVER MY LIFE, OUR CHURCH HAS BEEN SO IMPORTANT IN HELPING ME, NOT ONLY TO ACCEPT CHRIST, BUT ALSO TO LEARN TO KNOW HIM SO MUCH BETTER. THE MANY KINDS OF MINISTRIES IN THE CHURCH HELP ME (and my family) GROW IN THE LORD."</td></tr>
</table>

Note: Remember, *you are continuing to earn the right to later ask them the real question,* concerning their relationship with God. Remember, too, that *the Holy Spirit is actively involved* in this situation and is extremely interested in the results.

(4) *Identify their personal relationship with God*

You will be dealing with prospects in one of four spiritual conditions:

- Those who profess to be Christians and *have a vital relationship with God*
  Requires public relations call
- Those who profess to be Christians but *do not have a vital relationship with God*
  Requires Born-again Presentation (p. 204)
- Those who *do not profess* to be Christians but are somewhat interested in the benefits of the Christian life.
  Requires Born-again Presentation (p. 204)
- Those who *are born-again Christians* and are *seeking the Spirit-filled life*
  Requires Spirit-filled Presentation (p. 206)

Notes

The following approach can be used in dealing with a person *in any one of the above spiritual conditions.*

KEY STATEMENT	"BILL OR JANE, IT HAS BEEN SO GREAT VISITING WITH YOU." (Wait for a response.)

KEY STATEMENT	"YOUR INTEREST IN SPIRITUAL THINGS IS EVIDENT IN OUR CONVERSATION." (Wait for a response.)

KEY QUESTION	(With great tenderness) "HAVE YOU EVER KNOWN CHRIST AS YOUR PERSONAL SAVIOR?" (Wait for a response.)

KEY QUESTION	"IS YOUR RELATIONSHIP WITH CHRIST MEANINGFUL AND SATISFYING TO YOU?"

Note: There are occasions when people will not be totally honest at this point, but this gives no reason to argue. It is better to win a person than a point. God knows their heart, and He can deal judgment or conviction—you can only manifest love and acceptance.

If their answer is *"YES,"* then your conversation becomes a *public relations visit,* and *proceed to find out how your church can better serve them.*

If their answer is *"NO,"* your next question is:

KEY QUESTION	"BILL OR JANE, I'M SURE YOU WOULD ALLOW ME TO SHARE SOME SCRIPTURE WITH YOU, WOULDN'T YOU?"

You then proceed with the "Presentation of the Born-again Life."

b. Approach No. 2—To prospects who have not attended your church

(1) *Identify their secular background*

(2) *Identify their church background*

(3) *Identify their personal relationship with God*

Note: You may use the same format as is used in Approach No. 1, with the exception of references to the church.

(Number 3 of Approach No. 1 has been deleted, as it deals with your own church, which they have not yet attended.)

2. Presentation for the Born-again Life

a. Divine Initiative

KEY QUESTION	"BILL OR JANE, DO YOU REALIZE THAT GOD IS REACHING OUT TO PEOPLE?"

The Scriptures declare:

KEY SCRIPTURES	**For God so loved** the world, that **he gave** his only begotten Son, that whosoever believeth in him should not perish, but have everlasting life.　*(John 3:16, KJV, emphases added)* But God commendeth his love toward us, in that, while we were yet sinners, Christ died for us.　*(Rom. 5:8, KJV)*

KEY STATEMENTS	"GOD KNOWS AND **LOVES YOU AND ME** VERY MUCH. HE HAS DESIGNED A SPECIAL PLAN FOR YOUR LIFE. ISN'T THAT EXCITING? 　"GOD HAS NOT WAITED FOR YOU TO REACH OUT TO HIM, BUT HE IS RIGHT NOW REACHING DOWN TO SAVE YOU FROM YOUR SINS AND SHARE WITH YOU HIS PLAN."

b. Awareness of Need

KEY QUESTION	"BILL OR JANE, DO YOU REALIZE THAT GOD HELPS PEOPLE RECOGNIZE THEIR SINFUL CONDITION?"

Paul clearly establishes the fact that all have sinned.

KEY SCRIPTURE	For all have sinned and fall short of the glory of God.　*(Rom. 3:23)*

(1) When we look around at our world, as great as it is, we are all aware that something is wrong.

(2) It is the work of the Holy Spirit to bring us to this awareness of sins.

KEY SCRIPTURE	And He [the Holy Spirit], when He comes, will convict the world concerning sin.　*(John 16:8, NASB)*

c. Awareness of Moral Choice

KEY QUESTION	"BILL OR JANE, DO YOU REALIZE YOUR GREATEST POWER IS THE POWER TO CHOOSE?"

The Bible is very clear in confronting man with the important fact of a moral choice.

KEY SCRIPTURE	**Whoever believes [puts his faith] in the Son** has eternal life, but **whoever rejects the Son** will not see [that] life, for God's wrath remains on him.　*(John 3:36, emphases added)*

It is an important moment when you recognize things in your life that are *not pleasing to God.* To simply realize they are wrong is not enough.

Many would like *for God or someone else* to make that moral choice for them. But that would reduce us to mechanical robots or machines. *The power to choose* that God gave us is our *greatest power.* However, with this great power comes *grave responsibility.*

d. Our Response

KEY QUESTION	"BILL OR JANE, DO YOU REALIZE THAT EVERYONE RESPONDS TO GOD ONE WAY OR ANOTHER?"

Everyone gives a response to God. Either we repent of our sins and accept Christ, or we reject God's loving call.

Christ is beautifully pictured in Revelation, saying,

KEY SCRIPTURE	Here I am! I stand at the door and knock. If anyone **hears my voice** and **opens the door,** I will come in and eat with him, and he with me. *(Rev. 3:20, emphases added)*

KEY QUESTION	"BILL OR JANE, YOU MAY ASK, 'HOW DO I OPEN THE DOOR?'"

John makes it very clear when he says,

KEY SCRIPTURE	**If we confess** our sins, he is faithful and just and **will forgive** us our sins and purify us from all unrighteousness. *(1 John 1:9, emphases added)*

KEY QUESTION	"BILL OR JANE, DOES THIS MAKE SENSE TO YOU?"

If their answer is *"NO,"* then you simply and softly say, "WHAT PART OF IT TROUBLES YOU?" Then you begin to deal with their questions systematically.

If their answer is *"YES,"* you then move to the next question.

KEY QUESTION	"BILL OR JANE, IS THERE ANY GOOD REASON WHY, RIGHT HERE IN THE PRIVACY OF THIS ROOM, YOU WOULDN'T WANT TO ACCEPT (or RENEW YOUR RELATIONSHIP WITH) JESUS CHRIST AS YOUR PERSONAL SAVIOR?"

If their answer is *"YES,"* remember, regardless of the reason, you are more interested in winning a person than a point. Therefore, if it is a matter of misunderstanding something, clear that up simply and softly; but if they are backing down, let them do so with warmth and continued acceptance.

If their answer is *"NO,"* simply recapitulate the presentation in no more than 60 seconds, and then suggest that you have a simple prayer together.

When they say *"NO,"* suggest that you pray a brief prayer of thanking God that Bill and Jane have decided to accept Christ; then *if they know how to pray,* suggest they follow your prayer—but if *they simply don't know how,* or would like some help in praying, then simply pray a prayer of confession, faith, and thanks for them, and ask them to repeat each phrase.

3. Follow-through and Discipleship After Presentation and Acceptance of the Born-again Life

a. *Forgiveness*

KEY QUESTION	"ISN'T IT A GREAT FEELING TO KNOW THAT YOUR SINS ARE FORGIVEN, AND THAT YOU HAVE BEEN PARDONED?"
KEY SCRIPTURE	If we confess our sins, he is faithful and just and will forgive us our sins and purify us from all unrighteousness. *(1 John 1:9)*

b. *Justification*

KEY STATEMENT	"BILL OR JANE, NOT ONLY HAS CHRIST FORGIVEN YOU, BUT ALSO YOU HAVE BEEN JUSTIFIED, WHICH MEANS YOU NOW STAND BEFORE GOD JUST AS IF YOU HAD NEVER SINNED."
KEY SCRIPTURE	God presented him as a sacrifice of atonement, through faith in his blood. He did this to demonstrate his justice, because in his forbearance he had left the sins committed beforehand unpunished. *(Rom. 3:25)*

c. Regeneration

KEY STATEMENT	"YOU HAVE BEEN FORGIVEN, JUSTIFIED, AND REGENERATED, WHICH MEANS, BILL OR JANE, YOU HAVE NOW RECEIVED **NEW LIFE** THROUGH CHRIST."

KEY SCRIPTURE	Therefore, if anyone is in Christ, he is a new creation; the old has gone, the new has come! *(2 Cor. 5:17)*

d. Adoption

KEY STATEMENT	"BILL OR JANE, YOU HAVE BEEN FORGIVEN, JUSTIFIED, REGENERATED, AND ALSO ADOPTED. YOU HAVE NOW BECOME A CHILD OF GOD."

KEY SCRIPTURE	The Spirit himself testifies with our spirit that we are God's children. Now if we are children, then we are heirs—heirs of God and co-heirs with Christ. *(Rom. 8:16-17)*

KEY QUESTION	"ISN'T IT A **GREAT FEELING** TO KNOW THAT YOU ARE A BORN-AGAIN CHRISTIAN?"

e. Involvement

KEY STATEMENT	"NOW THAT YOU HAVE BECOME A BORN-AGAIN CHRISTIAN, BILL OR JANE, THERE ARE TWO THINGS IN WHICH YOU SHOULD BECOME INVOLVED: (1) AN ACTIVE DISCIPLING GROUP, AND (2) A VITAL, DYNAMIC, SPIRITUAL CHURCH."

BRIEF EXPLANATION: Occasionally you will be dealing with a person who has *become aware of his or her need for the Spirit-filled experience.* Under the *direction of the Holy Spirit, prayerfully proceed* with the Presentation of the Spirit-filled Life. Included at this point, for *your convenience,* is a review of the qualifying procedure that was used previously.

1. IDENTIFY THEIR SECULAR BACKGROUND.
2. IDENTIFY THEIR CHURCH BACKGROUND.
3. IDENTIFY THEIR RELATIONSHIP WITH YOUR CHURCH.
4. IDENTIFY THEIR RELATIONSHIP TO GOD.
Note: Final Key Question is: "Bill or Jane, I'm sure you would allow me to share some scripture with you, wouldn't you?"

Review and be prepared to utilize the following diagrams as "tablet talk" while you present the Spirit-filled Life.

SIN

Sinful Acts	Sinful Nature
willful transgressions for which we are responsible	original sin in the heart for which we were not initially responsible

Born-again Life **or** **Conversion**	**Spirit-filled Life** **or** **Entire Sanctification**
A New Relationship In response to repentance, confession, and faith, committed sins are forgiven by God.	**A New Relationship** In response to complete consecration and faith, there is a cleansing of the inner self and an empowering for service.

"SELF-CENTERED HEART"   "CONFLICTED HEART"   "GOD-ENTHRONED HEART"

The Christian Experience

CRISIS	CONTINUATION		CRISIS	CONTINUATION
1. Divine Initiative 2. Awareness of Need 3. Awareness of Moral Choice 4. Your Response		CONFLICT	1. Divine Initiative 2. Awareness of Need 3. Awareness of Moral Choice 4. Your Response	ABSENCE OF CONFLICT
1. Forgiveness 2. Justification 3. Regeneration 4. Adoption	Confrontation and Temptation—Confrontation and Temptation		1. Heart Purity 2. Heart Perfection 3. Infilling of the Holy Spirit 4. Empowering of the Holy Spirit	Confrontation and Temptation, Etc., Etc.
BORN-AGAIN			SPIRIT-FILLED (Entirely Sanctified)	

4. Presentation for the Spirit-filled Life

a. *Divine Initiative*

KEY QUESTION	"BILL OR JANE, I HAVE SOME GREAT NEWS FOR YOU. DO YOU REALIZE THAT GOD HAS A PLAN WHEREBY YOU CAN BE FREE FROM THIS INNER CONFLICT THAT YOU SENSE IN YOUR LIFE?"
KEY SCRIPTURE	And so Jesus also suffered outside the city gate to make the people holy through his own blood. *(Heb. 13:12)*

b. *Awareness of Need*

KEY STATEMENT	"BILL OR JANE, THIS IS PERHAPS THE GREATEST DAY IN YOUR LIFE, BECAUSE YOU HAVE RECOGNIZED YOUR NEED FOR GOD TO DELIVER YOU FROM THIS SELFISH, SINFUL NATURE. CHRIST HAS PROMISED, THROUGH THE HOLY SPIRIT, TO MEET THIS NEED."
KEY SCRIPTURES	What a wretched man I am! Who will rescue me from this body of death? *(Rom. 7:24)* Blessed are they which do hunger and thirst after righteousness: for they shall be filled. *(Matt. 5:6, KJV)*

c. *Awareness of Choice*

KEY QUESTION AND STATEMENT	"BILL OR JANE, DO YOU REALIZE THAT YOUR GREATEST POWER IS YOUR POWER TO CHOOSE? (Wait for a response.) JUST AS YOU HAD TO MAKE A CHOICE TO ENTER INTO THE BORN-AGAIN LIFE, SO YOU ALSO HAVE TO MAKE A MORAL CHOICE TO RECEIVE A CURE FOR THE SELFISH, SINFUL NATURE."
KEY SCRIPTURE	But just as he who called you is holy, so be holy in all you do; for it is written: "Be holy, because I am holy." *(1 Pet. 1:15-16)*

d. *Man's Response*

KEY STATEMENT	"NOT ONLY IS GOD **REACHING OUT** TO YOU AND HELPING YOU **BECOME AWARE** OF YOUR NEED, BUT ALSO, BILL OR JANE, YOU HAVE THE PRIVILEGE OF RESPONDING TO YOUR SPIRITUAL NEED BY:
	        presenting yourself as a living sacrifice to God,
	                    and also
	        accepting the infilling and cleansing power of the Holy Spirit."

KEY SCRIPTURE	I beseech you therefore, brethren, by the mercies of God, that ye present your bodies a living sacrifice, holy, acceptable unto God, which is your reasonable service. *(Rom. 12:1, KJV)*

KEY STATEMENT AND QUESTION	"BILL OR JANE, THIS WONDERFUL GIFT OF THE HOLY SPIRIT CAN BE YOURS TODAY, SIMPLY BY:
	    acknowledging your need
	    confessing this need to God
	    committing everything you are and have to God
	    believing that God accepts your commitment and cleanses and infills you **NOW** with the Holy Spirit.
	BILL OR JANE, DOES THIS MAKE SENSE TO YOU?"

If their first answer is *"NO,"* then you simply and softly ask, "WHAT PART OF IT TROUBLES YOU?" Then you begin to deal with their questions systematically.

If their answer is *"YES,"* then you move to the next question.

KEY QUESTION	"BILL OR JANE, IS THERE ANY GOOD REASON WHY, RIGHT HERE IN THE PRIVACY OF THIS ROOM, YOU WOULDN'T WANT TO ACCEPT THIS SPIRIT-FILLED LIFE?"

If their answer is *"YES,"* remember that, regardless of the reason, you are more interested in winning a person than a point. Therefore, if it is a matter of misunderstanding something, clear that up simply and softly, perhaps with the use of another one of the diagrams. But if they seem to be backing down, let them do so with warmth and continued acceptance.

If their answer is *"NO,"* simply review the presentation in no more than 60 seconds, and then suggest that you have a simple prayer together. Inasmuch as Bill and Jane are already Christians, they will probably have no difficulty praying. However, if there is any hesitation, lead them in a prayer of *acknowledgment, confession, commitment, faith,* and *thanks.*

5. Follow-through and Discipleship After Presentation and Acceptance of the Spirit-filled Life

a. Heart Purity

KEY QUESTION	"ISN'T IT A GREAT **FEELING** TO **KNOW** THAT ALL OF THE POLLUTION AND CORRUPTION FROM YOUR OLD SINFUL NATURE HAS BEEN CLEANSED?"

KEY SCRIPTURE	He made no distinction between us and them, for he **purified their hearts by faith.** *(Acts 15:9, emphasis added)*

b. Heart Perfection

KEY STATEMENT	"BILL OR JANE, GOD NOT ONLY HAS **PURIFIED YOUR HEART** BUT ALSO HAS **RESTORED HIS** MORAL NATURE IN YOU. HE HAS PERFECTED YOUR AFFECTIONS AND MOTIVES."

KEY SCRIPTURES	Be perfect, therefore, as your heavenly Father is perfect. *(Matt. 5:48)* and Herein is our **love made perfect,** that we may have boldness in the day of judgment: because as he is, so are we in this world. *(1 John 4:17, KJV, emphasis added)*

c. Infilling of the Holy Spirit

KEY STATEMENT	"ONE OF THE EXCITING FACTS ABOUT THE SPIRIT-FILLED LIFE IS THAT HE COMES IN AND COMPLETELY FILLS YOUR HEART, BILL OR JANE. THIS MEANS THAT THE MORAL CONFLICT IS GONE, AND THE HOLY SPIRIT **ABIDES, COMFORTS,** AND **ASSISTS** YOU IN YOUR SPIRITUAL GROWTH."

KEY SCRIPTURE	And he shall give you another Comforter, that he may abide with you for ever; . . . for he dwelleth with you, and shall be in you. *(John 14:16-17, KJV)*

d. Empowering of the Holy Spirit

KEY QUESTION	"BILL OR JANE, DURING THE TIME YOU EXPERIENCED THE BORN-AGAIN LIFE, DID YOU EVER WISH THAT YOU HAD MORE **POWER** TO LIVE THAT LIFE CONSISTENTLY?" (Wait for a response.)

KEY STATEMENT	"THE THRILLING FACT ABOUT THE SPIRIT-FILLED LIFE IS THAT, WHEN THE SPIRIT COMES IN TO ABIDE, HE **FURNISHES THE POWER** NECESSARY TO LIVE A **VICTORIOUS LIFE.** THIS SPIRITUAL POWER IS POSSIBLE BECAUSE OF: an absence of moral conflict in the cleansed heart and the indwelling presence of the Holy Spirit, who is your **POWER SOURCE.**"

KEY SCRIPTURE	But you will receive power when the Holy Spirit comes on you. *(Acts 1:8)*

KEY STATEMENTS

"BILL OR JANE, WITHOUT DOUBT, THIS IS THE **GREATEST DAY** IN YOUR SPIRITUAL DEVELOPMENT.

YOU NOW KNOW CHRIST AS YOUR **SAVIOR** AND **LORD.**

NOW THAT YOU HAVE BECOME SPIRIT-FILLED, BILL OR JANE, THERE ARE TWO THINGS IN WHICH YOU SHOULD BECOME INVOLVED:

(1) AN ACTIVE DISCIPLING GROUP, AND

(2) A VITAL, DYNAMIC, SPIRITUAL CHURCH.

I WOULD LIKE TO MAKE MYSELF AVAILABLE TO YOU TO HELP YOU IN ANY WAY I CAN AS YOU BECOME AN INVOLVED, SPIRIT-FILLED CHRISTIAN."

Conclusion

In this study, *Today's Disciple,* the "Mandate of the Master" ("go and make disciples") has been aimed at helping you . . .

- Understand
- Experience
- Communicate

. . . the dynamics of the Christian life.

As you will recall, this material has been developed from the standpoint of "Discipling Building Blocks."

Share	**Personal Evangelism**
	Priorities　**Temptation**
Growth	**Commitment**　**Obedience**
	Faith　**Prayer**　**God's Will**
Solution	**Spirit-filled Life**
	Born-again Life
Problem	**The Human Experience**
Basis	**The Word of God**
Premise	**Mandate of the Master**

If you have approached these 13 chapters with a "learner's heart," you will find a rewarding experience in looking back at the *you* who began chapter 1, and the *you* who has completed this final chapter. Pause right now and . . .

> THANK GOD FOR
> YOUR SPIRITUAL
> GROWTH

This is your final exercise of this study. Write in the box below:

Five areas of growth that can be attributed to the Holy Spirit's use of *Today's Disciple.*

1. _____

2. _____

3. _____

4. _____

5. _____